# ?
# HOW

## Comparing
## Places

# Teacher's
# Guide

Trudy Boyle

**Heinemann**

Heinemann Educational
A Division of Heinemann Educational Books Ltd,
Halley Court, Jordan Hill, Oxford OX2 8EJ

OXFORD  LONDON  EDINBURGH
MADRID  ATHENS  BOLOGNA  PARIS
MELBOURNE  SYDNEY  AUCKLAND  SINGAPORE
TOKYO  IBADAN  NAIROBI  HARARE
GABORONE  PORTSMOUTH NH (USA)

© Trudy Boyle, 1993
published by Heinemann Educational

First published 1993

93 94 95 96 97 98 10 9 8 7 6 5 4 3 2 1

Designed by Miller, Craig and Cocking
Illustrated by Hardlines

Typeset by Stables Typesetting, Swindon
Printed in Great Britain by Athenæum Press Limited,
Newcastle upon Tyne

ISBN 0435 04295 5

Original development work for the
**Heinemann Our World** series was done by
the University of Leeds Curriculum
Development Project.

The extracts from *Geography in the National
Curriculum* are reproduced with the
permission of the Controller of Her Majesty's
Stationery Office.

Cover photograph courtesy of South
American Pictures/Tony Morrison (to whom
thanks are due for his help on the sections on
Manaus).

Series adviser: Bill Boyle, CFAS, School of
Education, Manchester University

# CONTENTS

# Introduction to HEINEMANN OUR WORLD

**Heinemann Our World** is an innovative topic-based approach to teaching the National Curriculum at Key Stages 1 and 2. It is designed to help you to address all the National Curriculum requirements for Geography, History, Science and Technology.

The series comprises 33 individual topics, each providing ample ideas and materials for about half a term's work. Each topic is complete in itself and can be used independently of the others. There are 10 topics focusing primarily on Geography, 8 topics focusing on History and 15 on Science and Technology.

## Comprehensive coverage

To ensure that children develop the concepts and skills necessary for each subject, each topic focuses on one or two subjects. This topic focuses on Geography alone, but work in other National Curriculum core and foundation subjects and the cross-curricular themes has been integrated where appropriate.

Coverage of the National Curriculum across the topics has been carefully mapped to ensure that there is progression and variation in learning experiences and to provide ample opportunities for children to revisit key concepts. The topics for Key Stage 1 focus on Levels 1–3, with the emphasis being on Levels 1 and 2. Levels 2–5 are covered at Key Stage 2. Progression has been built into the topics focusing on Geography for Key Stage 2 as shown below:

| Topic | Level |
|---|---|
| People Live Here | 2, with some 3 |
| Looking Around | 2, with some 3 |
| Our Local Community | 2–3, with some 4 |
| Here and There | 3, with some 2 and 4 |
| Where You Live | 3, with some 2 and 4 |
| Comparing Places | 4, with some 3 and 5 |
| Looking at our Environment | 4, with some 3 and 5 |

The **Heinemann Our World** materials are designed to reduce the pressures on teachers' time; through providing an integrated yet flexible approach to teaching the National Curriculum, the materials enable teachers to continue to plan and teach to meet the particular needs of their class.

## Promoting skills development

Throughout the materials, children are encouraged to ask questions, to find answers for themselves and to solve problems. Many of the activities are designed to encourage children to work collaboratively. This not only helps them to acquire knowledge and concepts, but also to develop speaking, listening, cognitive and social skills.

In every topic there is a balance of activities between those requiring direction by the teacher and those that children can tackle on their own, either individually or in groups. These latter 'child-led' activities are supported by materials which can be used independently of the teacher.

## Supporting the teacher

Whilst group activity work encourages children to work independently, the teacher's role is still very important. The **Teacher's Guides** give guidance on how and when teacher intervention, support and assistance might be beneficial.

## In-built assessment

Assessment is continuous and fully integrated in **Heinemann Our World**. Opportunities for assessment are clearly highlighted in the **Teacher's Guides**, with the relevant **Statements of Attainment** indicated and suggestions for evidence of achievement given. Assessment is achieved through a variety of means: observation, questions and evaluation of work produced by the children.

We hope that you will enjoy using the material provided in this and other **Heinemann Our World** topics. A full list of geography topics is provided on page 80.

# Introduction to COMPARING PLACES

**Comparing Places** is designed to be used with upper juniors and focuses on Level 4 of the National Curriculum, with some coverage of Levels 3 and 5.

The topic focuses on Geography, but includes links to Maths, English, History and Science, as well as to the cross-curricular themes of Economic and Industrial Understanding, Environmental Education and Health Education.

## Ideas underlying the topic

- Children need to develop knowledge and understanding of the geography of where they live and of other places in the United Kingdom and abroad.

- Children can develop their skills by studying geographical themes through place studies.

- Activities should take account of children's interests, experience and capabilities.

- Children should encounter a range of planned activities, structured to include progression and continuity in the knowledge, skills and attitudes which the topic aims to address.

- Children benefit socially and educationally from participating in structured activities with a partner or in small groups.

- Teaching approaches and organizational strategies should be selected to suit the aims of each particular activity.

## How are these ideas provided for in this topic?

- By studying the geographical features and activities of the cities of Bristol (England) and Manaus (Brazil).

- By studying the geographical factors related to the changes that have taken place in Bristol and Manaus.

- By developing skills such as using Ordnance Survey maps, drawing sketch maps, and identifying features on aerial photos within these two place studies.

- By collaboratively debating, and developing proposals for, topics such as changes in land use.

## What does the topic aim to address?

The topic focuses on aspects of **Geography Attainment Targets 1, 2, 4** and **5**.

The work on **Attainment Target 1** focuses on:

- using four-figure co-ordinates in locating features on a map

- measuring the straight-line distance between two points on a plan

- identifying features on a large-scale map and a vertical air photo of the same place

- using an index and a contents page of an atlas

- drawing a sketch map using symbols and a key.

The work on **Attainment Target 2** focuses on:

- identifying features of the local area and using correct geographical vocabulary to name these features

- comparing features of the local area with other localities as specified in the Programmes of Study

- explaining the relationship between types of land use, buildings and human activities in the local area

- describing how the landscape of a locality outside the local area has been changed by human actions.

The work on **Attainment Target 4** focuses on:

- giving reasons for ways in which land is used and for the location of different types of economic activity

- explaining why different forms of transport are used

- explaining why shortest transport routes are not always in straight lines.

The work on **Attainment Target 5** focuses on:

- describing effects on environments of extracting natural resources

- identifying main sources of clean water and describing ways of ensuring a reliable supply.

**Geography Statements of Attainment addressed in the topic**

| Name of Activity | Key SOAs | Other SOAs which could be assessed | Links with other subject areas |
|---|---|---|---|
| 1. Discovering Bristol | 1/4a | 1/3c, 1/5c, 2/4a | Maths |
| 2. Discovering Manaus | 1/4a | 2/5a, 2/5b | Maths |
| 3. A bird's eye view of Bristol | 1/4c | 1/4f, 2/3f | |
| 4. Manaus from the air | 1/4c | 2/3d | |
| 5. Using your atlas to find Bristol | 1/4e | 1/3a | English |
| 6. Using your atlas to find Manaus | 1/4e | 2/3a, 2/4a | English |
| 7. Making a sketch map: Bristol | 1/4f | 1/3c, 2/3c, 2/3e | |
| 8. Sketching Manaus | 1/4f | 1/3c | |
| 9. Between two points: Bristol | 1/4b, 4/4d | 4/3c | |
| 10. Transport to and from Manaus | 1/4b, 4/4d | 2/4b, 4/5d | Maths |
| 11. Making changes: Bristol | 2/4b | 2/3c, 2/3d, 4/3d, 4/4e, 2/3e | History |
| 12. Changing times: Manaus | 4/3c, 2/4b | 2/3d, 2/3f, 4/5c | Science |
| 13. How Bristol is changing | 2/4b | 1/4f, 2/3c | History |
| 14. The changing face of Manaus | 2/4b, 2/3d | 4/4e, 4/5c | EIU |
| 15. Using land in Bristol | 4/4e | 1/3d, 4/3d, 2/3e, 2/3f | EIU |
| 16. City patterns: Manaus | 4/4e | 4/3d, 1/4f | |
| 17. Natural resources: Bristol | 5/3a, 5/3b | 4/4e, 2/3f, 5/5b | Environmental Ed. |
| 18. Vanishing forest: Manaus | 5/3a, 5/4b | 1/4e, 5/5b | Environmental Ed. |
| 19. Water supply: Bristol | 5/4a | 2/3d | Health Ed. |
| 20. Water supply: Manaus | 5/4a | 2/3d | Health Ed. |
| 21. Comparing Bristol and Manaus | 2/3c, 2/3d | 2/4b, 1/4e, 1/3b | Art and Design, English, Environmental Education |

EIU = Economic and Industrial Understanding

# Planning the use of the topic

## Overview

The sections are organized in pairs, with one spread on Bristol and one on Manaus. This enables comparisons to be made between the two places, and provides opportunities to reinforce the same skills in different contexts.

In Sections 1 and 2 the emphasis is on recognizing geographical features and using letter/number co-ordinates or four-figure co-ordinates to locate features on a map.

In Sections 3 and 4 the work focuses on using vertical air photos in conjunction with maps and drawing sketch maps using symbols and a key.

Sections 5 and 6 concentrate on how atlases can be used to access geographical information, in particular the use of the index and contents page.

In Sections 7 and 8 the emphasis is on identifying geographical features on maps, drawing sketch maps and creating keys to explain symbols.

In Sections 9 and 10 the children use a scale to measure distances accurately. Through doing so they will realize that a straight line route between places is not always possible.

In Sections 11 and 12 children are asked to note landscape changes and to classify these changes as human or natural. Sections 13 and 14 extend this work and children are asked to consider whether these changes are planned or unplanned.

The focus of Sections 15 and 16 is on land use and the reasons for land use in specific locations. Further work on using aerial photos is provided.

The focus of Sections 17 and 18 is on the range of natural resources that can be obtained from the environment. Children are asked to identify which natural resources are obtained in their local area, the processes for extraction of these resources and the effect of the extraction processes on the environment.

Main sources of clean water and how clean water supplies can be attained are the focal point of Sections 19 and 20.

In the final section, features and activities of your local area are compared with those of Bristol and Manaus.

## Structure and flexibility within the topic

For each section a number of central learning opportunities drawn from the Geography Programmes of Study and the Non-Statutory Guidance have been identified. The sections have been ordered to promote continuity and progression of the knowledge, skills and attitudes addressed in the topic. You may wish to choose from the sections when planning your teaching, and perhaps devise additional activities to go alongside the activities suggested in this Guide.

Most of the classroom activities can be conducted in the classroom itself. Some of the activities will benefit from fieldwork within the school grounds and the local area. These have been indicated in the Teacher's Guide.

### Time

The topic can either be covered with intensive teaching in half a term, or spread over an entire term. The sections can be adapted to suit the time available. For each section, extension and variation activities have been given, and the sections have been designed so that tasks can be revisited several times.

# Preparing for your teaching

## Resources provided

The chart on page 8 provides a summary of the materials provided for the topic. The materials consist of the pupil textbook (six copies of which are provided in the Topic Starter Pack) and activity sheets which are included in this Guide.

### Pupil book

Each spread in the pupil book forms a mini-unit of work. In addition to photos, maps and easy-to-read text providing a stimulus for the activities, the spreads each have a 'Things to do' box, providing tasks for the children to do either independently or with a partner or small group.

Ways of extending the tasks presented in the pupil book are suggested in the sections in this Guide.

On pages 46–48 of the pupil book there is a glossary of geographical terms.

### Activity sheets

There are 24 activity sheets. Some of these have maps of the places studied in the topic. Others provide the stimulus for follow-up or extension activities. Many of the activity sheets are linked to a specific Statement of Attainment and can be used for assessment. A record keeping chart for teacher use is provided on pages 78–9.

## Overview of resources provided

| Name of Section | Relevant textbook pages | Activity Sheets |
|---|---|---|
| 1. Discovering Bristol | 4–5 | 1, 2 |
| 2. Discovering Manaus | 6–7 | 3 |
| 3. A bird's eye view of Bristol | 8–9 | 4, 5 |
| 4. Manaus from the air | 10–11 | 6 |
| 5. Using your atlas to find Bristol | 12–13 | 7 |
| 6. Using your atlas to find Manaus | 14–15 | |
| 7. Making a sketch map: Bristol | 16–17 | 8, 9 |
| 8. Sketching Manaus | 18–19 | 10, 11 |
| 9. Between two points: Bristol | 20–21 | 12 |
| 10. Transport to and from Manaus | 22–23 | 13 |
| 11. Making changes: Bristol | 24–25 | 14, 15, 16 |
| 12. Changing times: Manaus | 26–27 | |
| 13. How Bristol is changing | 28–29 | 17 |
| 14. The changing face of Manaus | 30–31 | |
| 15. Using land in Bristol | 32–33 | 18 |
| 16. City patterns: Manaus | 34–35 | 19 |
| 17. Natural resources: Bristol | 36–37 | 20 |
| 18. Vanishing forest: Manaus | 38–39 | 21 |
| 19. Water supply: Bristol | 40–41 | 22 |
| 20. Water supply: Manaus | 42–43 | |
| 21. Comparing Bristol and Manaus | 44–45 | 23, 24 |

### Other resources

The activities in this topic make use of resources usually available in a typical primary classroom. The following list should be helpful in your preparations for teaching the topic.

### Art materials

Drawing materials (e.g. wax crayons, felt pens, pencil crayons, pastels)
Scissors
White paper, drawing and ruled
Range of coloured papers and card
Glue (PVA and paper glue)

### Further materials

Camera, film
Ordnance Survey maps
Range of local maps: as wide a variety as possible of old and modern, and to different scales (to include street maps and tourist maps)
Photos of features in the local area, different types of transport and goods and services
Maps, photos and tourist brochures from Brazil, in particular Manaus, and from Bristol

See also the list of books and other resources on page 80.

## Preparing your classroom

Throughout the topic the children will be producing material which can be used to create an evolving display. This display can be enhanced by the addition of material collected by you or the children.

Some suggestions of things to collect are given below:

- large-scale maps of the local area

- Ordnance Survey extracts

- oblique and vertical aerial photos (if possible correlated to map sections of the local area)

- a range of modern atlases

- examples of sketch maps with keys

- motorway network maps

- plans and any other photocopiable material from your local planning department

- material about the Amazonia region in general, or more specifically about Manaus

- details about Brazil's other major cities or regions

- information on Bristol, e.g. maritime past, slave trade, modern development plans, etc.

## Ideas for sharing the topic

At the end of the topic, you and the children may wish to share the information you have researched with others. Your audience could be other children in the school, the head teacher or parents and other people from the community. Another possibility is to 'twin' with a school in the Bristol area and exchange project books.

The methods used to share the information with others could be equally varied. You could:

- invite people to the classroom to see the displays

- put up a display elsewhere (e.g. sometimes local building societies and other shops allow schools to put up displays in their windows)

- put on a presentation, either during an assembly or elsewhere

- write books about the places studied.

# SECTION: EACH SECTION HAS A NAME AND NUMBER

## Relevant pages for the pupil book are given in the margin.

## Relevant activity sheets are given in the margin.

The photocopy symbol also appears on relevant pages of the pupil book.

## Learning Opportunities

For each section a number of learning opportunities are identified. These are drawn from the National Curriculum Programmes of Study and Non-Statutory Guidance.
The learning opportunities are a selection of the ones that could have been chosen.

## Background Information

Information is given about the localities studied and about the geographical skills and concepts to be developed.

## Teaching and Learning Notes

Most of the sections are divided into two to four tasks. For each task details of what the task consists of are given, including advice on practical issues, how you might interact with the children and the sorts of ideas that the children will need to consider.

## Extensions and Variations

This part provides suggestions on how you might extend the section to cover further geographical skills and ideas or cross-curricular themes.

| Assessment opportunites | Statements of Attainment | Evidence of attainment | Bases of assessment |
|---|---|---|---|
| For each activity **Key SoAs** and **Other SoAs which could be assessed** are given. | Written out in full for your convenience. | What to look for to judge whether the child has achieved this SoA. | How the assessment is done, e.g. Oral. |

# Assessment

The chart on page 10 explains the design of the sections. As can be seen, the assessment opportunities for each task have been clearly indicated.

We have identified the assessment opportunities, suggested a method of assessment and indicated criteria for mastery to aid your assessment of each activity. Remember, these activities do not claim to provide definitive judgements on the children's attainments. They do, however, provide guidance to acceptable performance indicators for SoA related activities and as such will inform your planning for future teaching in geography. *When* you manage your assessment of the children and *who* you assess (i.e. whether you assess in a group or individually) has been left open, so that you can

choose the time and group size which best suits your children, your way of teaching and the purposes of your assessment.

For example, *formative*, or on-going assessments of the child's work can be made to decide whether (s)he needs more experience of an activity or needs a different type of activity.

If you are making a *summative* assessment you may decide to do so after a child has had a number of opportunities to consolidate their learning.

A summary of the Statements of Attainment addressed in the topic is provided on page 6. Your school may have already produced a record-keeping chart for Geography. Alternatively, you can use the charts on page 78–9.

# 1: DISCOVERING BRISTOL

## Learning Opportunities

There are opportunities for children to develop the understanding, skills and attitudes involved in:

▲ recognizing human and physical geographical features

▲ using four-figure co-ordinates to locate features on a map

▲ working with Ordnance Survey maps

▲ making a map of a short route

## Background Information

Bristol is one of the largest cities in the United Kingdom. Its beginnings as a settlement are not accurately known, although there was a Saxon settlement called Brigstow in this location around AD500. This name in Saxon means 'meeting place near a bridge'. Brigstow was situated between the rivers Avon and Frome, on high ground as a protection from flooding.

When the Normans invaded the area around AD1070 they built a castle on the site. Later, Bristol grew in fame and wealth due to its ideal position as a port on the Atlantic-facing west coast. (More historical information about Bristol is given on page 32.)

## Teaching and Learning Notes

### 1. Locating features

Discuss with the children the photos shown on page 4 of the pupil book. What human and physical features do they show? What do they tell us about Bristol?

The tasks on this spread provide an opportunity to introduce Ordnance Survey maps. The map on page 5 is 1:50,000; in other words, one centimetre on the map represents 500 metres (or 50,000 centimetres) on the ground. Discuss the simpler symbols with the children.

Make sure that the children can see/read the figures for the co-ordinates. They will probably already have been introduced to using letter/number co-ordinates to locate features on maps (a Level 3 skill). This activity focuses on the Level 4 requirement of using four-figure co-ordinates for locational purposes. To give the co-ordinates of a feature,

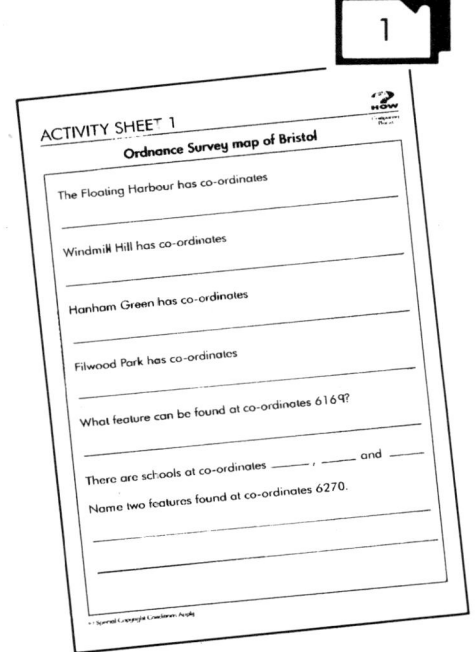

ACTIVITY SHEET 1

**Ordnance Survey map of Bristol**

The Floating Harbour has co-ordinates

Windmill Hill has co-ordinates

Hanham Green has co-ordinates

Filwood Park has co-ordinates

What feature can be found at co-ordinates 6169?

There are schools at co-ordinates ——— , ——— and ———

Name two features found at co-ordinates 6270.

---

| Assessment opportunities | Statements of Attainment |
|---|---|
| KEY SoA: Gg1/4a | Use four figure co-ordinates to locate features on a map |

Other SoAs which could be assessed:

| | |
|---|---|
| Gg1/3c | Make a map of a short route, showing features in the correct order |
| Gg1/5c | Follow a route on a 1:50 000 or 1:25 000 OS map and describe the features that would be seen |
| Gg2/4a | Name the features marked on Maps B and D at the end of the Programmes of Study* |
| | * Partial SoA (ALL would be required during the course of Key Stage 2 work.) |

first find the square in which it is located. Then give the number of the vertical line on the left of the feature ('Easting') and then the number of the horizontal line ('Northing') below the feature. The lines meet in the lower left-hand corner of the square. The first task asks the children to find the co-ordinates of the two places shown in the photos on page 4. The correct co-ordinates are as follows:

Temple Meads    5972     Floating Harbour    5772

The children can record their answers to all the tasks on this spread on Activity Sheet 1: *Ordnance Survey map of Bristol*.

## 2. More co-ordinates work

Note: this task relates to questions 2–5 in the pupil book. The correct co-ordinates for the places mentioned are as follows:

*Question 2*
*Windmill Hill 5971 Hanham Green 6470, 6471 Filwood Park 5969*
*Question 3*
Flowers Hill can be found at co-ordinates 6169.
*Question 4*
Schools can be found at co-ordinates 5870, 5940, 6069 and 6269.
*Question 5*
The two features found at co-ordinates 6270 are the college and the cemetery (the children might also identify the government buildings).

# Extensions and Variations

Use Activity Sheet 2: *Map of the United Kingdom* to locate where Bristol is in relation to your local area. This map shows the place names to be learned for Gg2/4a, of which Bristol is one.

    The children could practise using four-figure co-ordinates with an OS map of the local area. They could work in pairs to see how quickly each partner can name familiar local landmarks when given the local co-ordinates.

    To give the children further experience of using OS maps you could ask them to draw a route from two points on the Bristol map, e.g. from Hanham Green to Netham. Their route should show at least five features in the correct order.

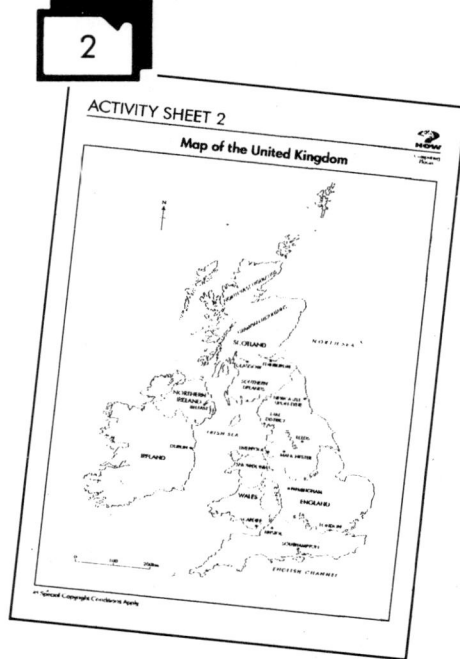

| Evidence of attainment | Bases of assessment |
| --- | --- |
| Child locates features from co-ordinates | Written |
| Child shows at least 3 features in plan view and in correct sequence | Product/Written |
| Child uses features shown on OS map to draw a route from Hanham Green to Netham. The route should show at least five of the following features (in the correct order): Broad, buildings, river, tunnel, Broom Hill, railway line, river loop (meander), park, River Netham. | Product/Written |
| Child identifies the places and features named on Activity Sheet 2 (Map D) | Written/Oral |

# 2: DISCOVERING MANAUS

## Learning Opportunities

There are opportunities for children to develop the understanding, skills and attitudes involved in:

▲ recognizing human and physical features
▲ using four-figure co-ordinates to locate features on a map
▲ exploring transport routes in Brazil
▲ identifying features on a map of the world

## Background Information

Brazil is the sixth largest country in the world with a population of 145 million. Most of its people live in the south and east, leaving the Amazon rainforest, which covers much of the centre and north, comparatively uninhabited. The total population of the rainforest is approximately 20 to 25 million.

There are five regions in Brazil: North, North-East, South-East, South and Central West. Each region comprises between three and ten states. Manaus is in the Amazonas State in the North Region, and is situated at the confluence of the River Amazon with its major tributary, the Rio Negro. The vast area of the Amazon rainforest which covers the Amazon river and its tributaries, and which extends into Colombia, Ecuador, Peru and Bolivia, is known as Amazonia. Manaus is both the state capital of Amazonas and the largest city in Amazonia with well over one million inhabitants. Many of these people have recently moved into the city, attracted by the prospect of work in the large electronics factories which have been set up by multinational companies in response to tax incentives from the Brazilian government.

## Teaching and Learning Notes

### 1. Introducing Brazil

If the children have heard about Brazil, it may be through football or television wildlife programmes on the destruction of the rainforest. Discuss what they have heard about the latter, e.g. scientific views that the cutting down of tracts of rainforest is a major contributory factor to the 'greenhouse effect' and global warming. Introduce the map of South America on page 6 of the pupil book and discuss with the children the location of Brazil in relation to the other countries in South America. You may like to use Activity Sheet 3: *Map of the world* to place Brazil in a

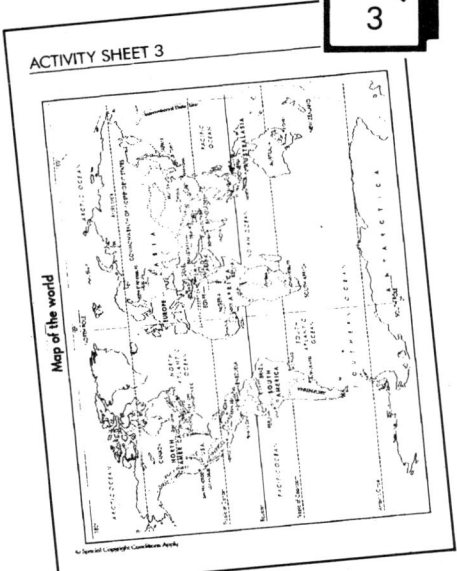

3

ACTIVITY SHEET 3

Map of the world

| Assessment opportunities | Statements of Attainment |
|---|---|
| *KEY SoA:*    Gg1/4a | Use four figure co-ordinates to locate features on a map |
| *Other SoAs which could be assessed:* | |
|    Gg2/5a | Name the features marked on Maps E and F at the end of the Programmes of Study* |
|    Gg2/5b | Describe how the characteristic features of the home region are interrelated |
| | *Partial SoA |

world context. (This map contains all the features from Mop F in the Programmes of Study.) While the children do not need to be able to name the features until Level 5, they should have opportunities to become familiar with (some of) them at this stage.

Ask the children to make a list of the main cities they can see on the map of Brazil on page 7 of the pupil book. In addition to Manaus, there are a number of cities in Brazil with a population over one million. These are: Brasilia, the capital (11 million); São Paulo (7 million); Rio de Janeiro (5 million); Salvador (11-12 million); Belo Horizonte (11-12 million); Recife (12 million) and Porto Alegre (11 million).

### 2. The Amazon

The Amazon can also be located and its relationship to the position of Manaus discussed. At about 6,400km, the Amazon is the second longest river in the world (the Nile is the longest), and the largest by volume. In some places it is 10km wide, and its deepest reaches go down 60m. It rises in Peru about 160km from the Pacific Ocean, and is known by several different names as it passes through various countries on its way to the Atlantic.

### 3. Locating Manaus on the map

If the children have not already found Manaus on the map, they should do so now. Ask them to give the correct co-ordinates (2644).

### 4. Finding co-ordinates

The children can practise using co-ordinates to find the following:
Rio de Janeiro    (2841)
Brasilia    (2742)
Porto Alegre    (2740)

## Extensions and Variations

The regions of Brazil are shown on Map B. This presents an opportunity to discuss and define the extent of a 'region'. The concept of the 'home region' is a key geographical issue, introduced at Levels 4 and 5, and leading into Key Stage 3 work. The pupil's home region will cover a large area or an area of high population. Help the children to identify and describe the geographical features of their home region and to show how the characteristic features of the region are related, i.e., the links between physical features, population distribution and patterns of settlement.

| Evidence of attainment | Bases of assessment |
|---|---|
| Child notes location of cities using co-ordinates | Written |
| Child locates South America and Brazil (and teacher-determined number of other features) on a map of the world | Observation |
| Child identifies and describes geographical features of the home region and explores the links between them | Oral |

# 3: A BIRD'S EYE VIEW OF BRISTOL

## Learning Opportunities

There are opportunities for children to develop the understanding, skills and attitudes involved in:

▲  using vertical aerial photos to locate features

▲  using a map of a locality in conjunction with an aerial photo

▲  drawing a sketch map using symbols and a key

▲  identifying reasons why activities or features are located where they are

## Background Information

This section provides an opportunity for the children to match and identify features of Bristol using both a vertical aerial photo and a map. At this level it is important that the children are given regular practical opportunities to familiarize themselves with accessing the details of maps and photographs and in trying to understand them. They need to develop the basic geographical skills to identify features on both oblique and vertical aerial photos and on maps of their local area.

## Teaching and Learning Notes

### 1. Matching aerial view photo to map

The task asks the children to find the Temple Meads area on both the map and the aerial photo. On which did the children find it first? After they had found it on one, say the map, how did they go about finding it on the aerial photo? Which clues does each give? Ask the children what a vertical aerial photo shows you that a map doesn't, and vice versa.

---

*Assessment opportunities*    *Statements of Attainment*

KEY SoA:    Gg1/4c          Identify features of both a large scale map and a vertical air photograph of the same place

*Other SoAs which could be assessed:*

Gg1/4f          Draw a sketch map using symbols and a key

Gg2/3f          Explain why some activities in the local area are located where they are

## 2. Looking for features

The children should make a list of other features that can be found on both the aerial photo and the map. These can be recorded on Activity Sheet 4: *Identify the features*, which is a black and white reproduction of the photo on page 8 of the pupil book.

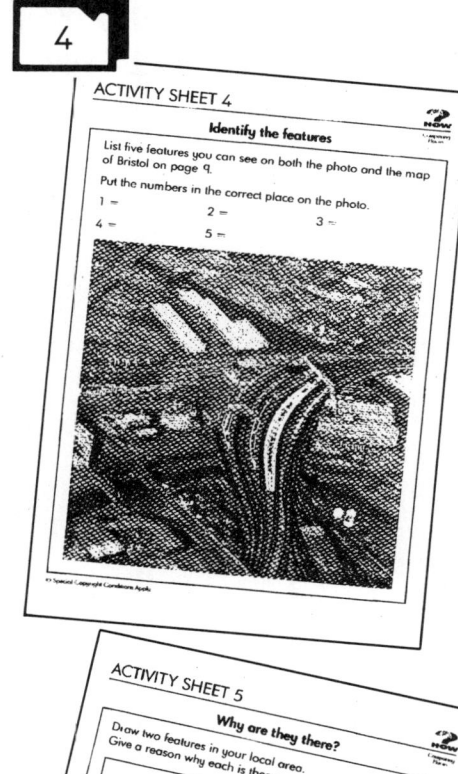

# Extensions and Variations

A comparison of aerial photos with maps leads naturally into a discussion of the use of keys on sketch maps. Children should be given aerial photos of other areas, preferably their local area or localities known to them. In pairs or small groups they should spend time identifying and selecting significant features and deciding on symbols which they may wish to include on a sketch map. Using one of these local aerial view photos they should draw their own sketch map using map symbols to identify the features and provide a useful key.

They could write some questions about their map and its aerial photo for another group to answer. This will help them to validate their sketch map and key.

Discuss ways in which Bristol is similar to or different from your local area. What features do they have in common? Move on to a discussion of why features in the local area are situated where they are, for example, an airport needs a large area of flat land; an out-of-town shopping centre needs to be easily accessible by transport. Activity Sheet 5: *Why are they there?* asks children to draw two features from the local area and to give reasons why they are where they are.

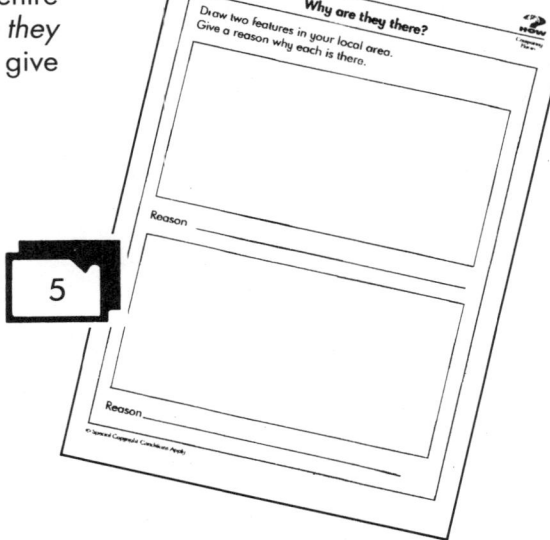

---

## Evidence of attainment

Child lists features shown on map and photo of Bristol

Child draws a sketch map of the local area showing features marked with appropriate symbols as shown in a key

Child draws two features from the local area and gives reasons why they are situated where they are

## Bases of assessment

Written

Product

Product/Written

## Learning Opportunities

There are opportunities for children to develop the understanding, skills and attitudes involved in:

▲ using vertical aerial photos to locate features

▲ using a map of a locality in conjunction with an aerial photo

▲ comparing features in Manaus with those in the local area

## Background Information

Manaus is the largest Amazonian city with a population that is growing rapidly. In 1960 the population was 165,000. It is now over 1 million. The city was originally built with the profits of the rubber industry. The Opera House (see map on page 11 of the pupil book) is a relic of this former prosperous era. Today, Manaus is a freeport with duty-free trading and government tax incentives for companies. The majority of its workforce are industrialized workers in the large electronics factories of the multinationals. Others work in the tourist industry, as Manaus is the centre for visitors to Amazonia.

## Teaching and Learning Notes

### 1. Locating features on a map

Discuss with the children the different features that they can see on the map on page 11 of the pupil book. Can they find the Customs offices, the Opera House (Teatro Amazonas), the Cathedral and the Floating Docks?

---

| *Assessment opportunities* | *Statements of Attainment* |
|---|---|
| KEY SoA:    Gg1/4c | Identify features on a large-scale map and on a vertical air photograph of the same place |
| *Other SoA which could be assessed:* | |
|             Gg2/3d | Compare features and occupations of the local area with other localities specified in the Programme of Study |

## 2. Comparing the aerial photo with the map

Having found the places in Question 1 on the map, the children should look for them in the photo on page 10 of the pupil book. Activity Sheet 6: *Features in Manaus* provides a black and white copy of the photo. The children should mark the photo to show where the buildings mentioned are. The Floating Docks, constructed at the turn of the century by British engineers, are in the foreground of the photograph. The Cathedral stands on its own, slightly to the right of centre halfway up the page. The Customs offices (consisting of the brown and ochre brick building – the Customs House – and the adjacent tall white tower) can be seen in the right-hand foreground above the docks. Manaus's splendid 19th century Opera House is visible to the left of the tower block, left of centre of the photograph.

## 3. Looking for other features

The children should go on to look for other features on the map and the photo. Through doing this task the children will become more familiar with the general layout and features of Manaus.

The places found can be marked on Activity Sheet 6, with an appropriate code.

## Extensions and Variations

Discuss what the children have found out about how people live in Manaus from the features that they have identified (e.g. what they can tell you about jobs, industry and housing). Compare their findings with your local area. A list of similarities and differences in the physical and human features and occupations of the two places should show at least four items to satisfy Gg2/3d – two similarities and two differences.

*Evidence of attainment*

Child lists features of Manaus

Child compares three features of Manaus with features in the local area

*Bases of assessment*

Product

Oral

# 5: USING YOUR ATLAS TO FIND BRISTOL

## Learning Opportunities

There are opportunities for children to develop the understanding, skills and attitudes involved in:

▲ recognizing how an atlas can be used to access a range of geographical information

▲ using an atlas to access a variety of information

▲ recognizing the routes to accessing specific information in an atlas

▲ recognizing the different classifications, sections and the information each will contain, in an atlas

▲ using letter/number co-ordinates to locate features on a map

## Background Information

Use a range of atlases from those providing simple pictorial access through to more sophisticated 'adult' versions to establish the progressive nature and range of uses of an atlas. We have used Philip's Children's Atlas in the illustration on pages 12 and 13 of the pupil book, and your school may well have other examples to offer. Which do the children think are easier to handle? Which would be most useful to them? Debate how they would decide on this. Try to establish the range of purposes for which an atlas might be needed by discussing what they are looking for and how easily that information can be accessed through the classification used in the atlas and the way it is presented.

## Teaching and Learning Notes

Before doing the Things To Do, discuss with the children how the contents page and index can be used to access information from an atlas.

### Contents page

What other kinds of books have they come across with contents pages? Discuss different purposes of contents lists. How is the contents page presented in the atlas they are using? Is it in sections? Explore simple classifications and categories. Do they understand the concept of geographical classifying? In other words, do they think the headings used in their atlas are good ways of arranging the information?

| *Assessment opportunities* | *Statements of Attainment* |
|---|---|
| KEY SoA: Gg1/4e | Use the index and contents pages to find information in an atlas |
| *Other SoA which could be assessed:* | |
| Gg1/3a | Use letter/number co-ordinates to locate features on a map |

## Index

Distinguish between an index and a gazetteer. An index is a list of names and concepts. Most of the names which are shown on the maps in the atlas are listed in the gazetteer. This is not always the rule in children's atlases, however. Look at the way the atlases you have available are arranged. Some atlases follow the style of countries and cities; others also name rivers, seas and lakes, mountains and deserts. All follow alphabetical order in the whole listing or in the separate sections. Use these suggestions to make a list of the things that you could use an index for in each of the atlases in your classroom.

Each place is listed by page and grid number. The letter/number co-ordinates grid is a Level 3 locational activity (Gg1/3a) but could provide a useful reinforcement.

The children should then use the atlas index on page 13 of the pupil book to find Belém, Belfast, Bethlehem and Birmingham.

## Extensions and Variations

Give the children further practice using the index to locate information in an atlas using those atlases available in the classroom. They could, for example, find the locations of places mentioned in the news.

Activity Sheet 7: *Letter/number co-ordinates* provides extra reinforcement for this skill (Gg1/3a). Where parts of the feature in question fall on more than one square, tell the children to give co-ordinates for the square that contains the name of the feature. It is important that the child correctly locates three places either in the course of the activity or on Activity Sheet 7, if Gg1/3a locational activity is to be attained. The location must be specified by giving the horizontal (letter) reference first in each case.

Sections 7 and 8 are concerned with making sketch maps. For the purposes of Geog 1/3c this means a map in plan view (i.e., not a pictorial map) with a clear starting and finishing point. The map should show at least three features in correct sequence, with at least one change of direction in the route.

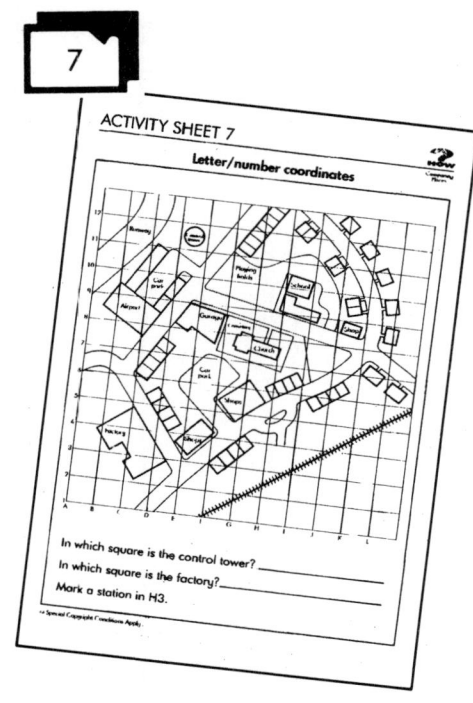

7

ACTIVITY SHEET 7

Letter/number coordinates

In which square is the control tower? _____
In which square is the factory? _____
Mark a station in H3.

---

## Evidence of attainment

Child uses contents page and index in atlas to access information on Bristol

Child locates at least three places/features using letter/number grid references or correctly fills in Activity Sheet 7

## Bases of assessment

Product

Product

# 6: USING YOUR ATLAS TO FIND MANAUS

## Learning Opportunities

There are opportunities for children to develop the understanding, skills and attitudes involved in:

▲ recognizing how an atlas can be used to access a range of geographical information

▲ using an atlas to access a variety of information

▲ recognizing the routes to accessing specific information in an atlas

▲ recognizing the different classifications, sections and the information each will contain, in an atlas

## Background Information

Children need to be given practical reasons for using atlases on a regular basis for them to become familiar with using them. You could, for example, start a collection of press cuttings from newspapers which mention places in the United Kingdom and abroad. The children could look for the places mentioned in the atlases and report what they have found to the rest of the class. Familiarity with atlases and maps in general will make it easier for children to be able to identify the features on Maps A and C (Gg2/3a) and Maps B and D (Gg2/4a) at the end of the Programmes of Study.

## Teaching and Learning Notes

### 1. Finding Manaus in an atlas

The children will already have located Manaus on a map of Brazil (Section 2). This task provides them with the opportunity to look for more maps showing Manaus in an atlas. Encourage the children to use both the contents page and the index/gazetteer to locate information.

### 2. Locating other Brazilian cities

Which Brazilian cities the children will find will vary, depending on what atlas they use. The children could compare the atlases available in the classroom. In which atlas are the most Brazilian cities shown? In which atlas are the least shown?

| Assessment opportunities | Statements of Attainment |
|---|---|
| KEY SoA:    Gg1/4e | Use the index and contents pages to find information in an atlas |
| Other SoAs which could be assessed: | |
| Gg2/3a | Name the features marked on Maps A and C at the end of the Programmes of Study* |
| Gg2/4a | Name the features marked on Maps B and D at the end of the Programmes of Study* |
| | *Partial SoA (During the Key Stage all the features should be correctly identified) |

### 3. Looking at atlases in more detail

Discuss with the children what other features can be found in an atlas. Do any of the atlases in the classroom have a gazetteer? What other types of maps are shown?

## Extensions and Variations

The children could work in groups to design their own atlas. They will need to decide what maps to include and in what order. They will then need to make up their own contents list and index. Discuss who will use the atlas, for example, what changes would they need to make if the atlas was to be used by children who might not be able to read as well as them? Explore concepts of pictorial context clues to cue in the subject of a page – the Statue of Liberty, for instance, might be used to evoke the map of the United States.

| *Evidence of attainment* | *Bases of assessment* |
|---|---|
| Child uses contents/index in atlas to access information on Manaus | Observation/Written/Product |
| Child correctly identifies all the features marked on the maps | Written/Oral |
| Child correctly identifies all the features marked on the maps | Written/Oral |

# 7: MAKING A SKETCH MAP: BRISTOL

## Learning Opportunities

There are opportunities for children to develop the understanding, skills and attitudes involved in:

▲ identifying features on maps, using correct geographical vocabulary

▲ drawing sketch maps to interpret these features

▲ creating symbols to indicate and represent features

▲ identifying the symbols by creating a key device

▲ making a map of a short route

▲ exploring the relationships between types of buildings and human activities

## Background Information

Although the skill of drawing a sketch map is not required until Level 4 (Gg1/4f), this activity should be seen as a progressive and coherent development from children's earlier representational activities. Opportunities for these are provided in Level 2 (Gg1/2b: make a representation of a real or an imaginary place) and Level 3 (Gg1/3c: make a map of a short route, showing features in the correct order).

It is important to remember that although this activity is at Level 4, the children are only required to create symbols, not use Ordnance Survey symbols. For assessment purposes, you should be expecting some indication of a movement towards using conventional symbols, but it is the ability to convey information in an accessible way, and to create and identify symbols on a child-produced key, which are the skills being assessed in Gg1/4f.

## Teaching and Learning Notes

### 1. Drawing a sketch map of Bristol

The children should draw a sketch map of a part of Bristol, using any of the maps and photos in the book for reference. Their product could be drawn on Activity Sheet 8: *Sketch map of Bristol*. Tell the children that their map is intended to guide tourists to some of the more interesting sights of Bristol (such as the Maritime Heritage Centre, Bristol Zoo, Exhibition Centre, Hands-on Science Centre, Industrial Museum, Cathedral, etc.). Discuss what these might be and how they could be represented with symbols. Before deciding on what symbols they will use, they will need to group and classify the features to be included.

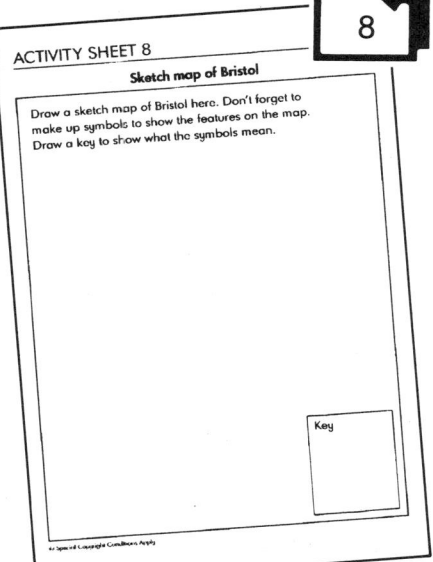

ACTIVITY SHEET 8

**8**

Sketch map of Bristol

Draw a sketch map of Bristol here. Don't forget to make up symbols to show the features on the map. Draw a key to show what the symbols mean.

Key

| Assessment opportunities | Statements of Attainment |
|---|---|
| KEY SoA    Gg1/4f | Draw a sketch map using symbols and a key |
| *Other SoAs which could be assessed:* | |
| Gg1/3c | Make a map of a short route, showing features in the correct order |
| Gg2/3c | Use correct geographical vocabulary to identify types of landscape features and activities with which they are familiar in the local area |
| Gg2/3e | Explain the relationships between types of land-use, buildings and human activities in the local area |

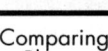

The children could go on to draw a recommended route for the tourists to follow, on their way from the station to an agreed point. The route should contain at least three features in the correct order.

## 2. Drawing a sketch map of the local area

This task provides a further opportunity to introduce and develop the drawing of geographical sketch maps. The activity will involve the children in exploring the local area on foot and noting features to be included on the map. This will lead into discussion of the features in the local area, why they are there and what they are used for. They will also need access to maps of the local area.

In preparation for drawing the sketch map, it might be useful for the children first to fill in Activity Sheet 9: *Features in the local area*, where they have to identify and name two local features and two local activities (such as delivering the post, swimming in a pool, working in offices, farming, etc.).

Suggest to the children that they make a focus map, for example, a map for tourists to their local area to show leisure or historical sites.

## Extensions and Variations

Using the children's own sketch maps of the local area, discuss with them why features (some human-made and some simple physical ones) are located where they are. Who uses the features they have drawn? Where do the users live in relation to the feature?

| Evidence of attainment | Bases of assessment |
|---|---|
| Child draws sketch map with key to explain the main symbols used on the map | Product |
| Child maps a route for tourists with three features in the correct order and one change in direction | Written/Oral |
| Child correctly names five local features to include on their sketch map | Written/Oral |
| Child identifies two local features and gives reasons for the location of each | Written/Oral |

# 8: SKETCHING MANAUS

## Learning Opportunities

There are opportunities for children to develop the understanding, skills and attitudes involved in:

▲ identifying features on maps
▲ drawing sketch maps to interpret these features
▲ creating symbols to indicate and represent features
▲ identifying the symbols by creating a key device
▲ drawing a map of a well-known route

## Background Information

This section presents an opportunity to develop an understanding of the concept of geographical features. 'Features' is one of the most used words in geography. It can refer to anything of geographical significance which can be classified as part of the natural (physical) environment, or part of the human (built) environment. Natural features would include hills, mountains and rivers. Human features include towns, reservoirs and motorways. By the end of Key Stage 2 children should be competent to make clear distinctions between features in the same category (e.g., residential roads and main roads, rail and air travel).

The most obvious natural feature of Manaus is the Rio Negro, with its inlets. The Cathedral, in the Spanish style, is a conspicuous human feature, as are the various skyscrapers built during the last twenty years. The winding streets of the old town around the port reveal their historic origins, while the strict grid plan of the rest of the town, suggests that it is of more recent construction.

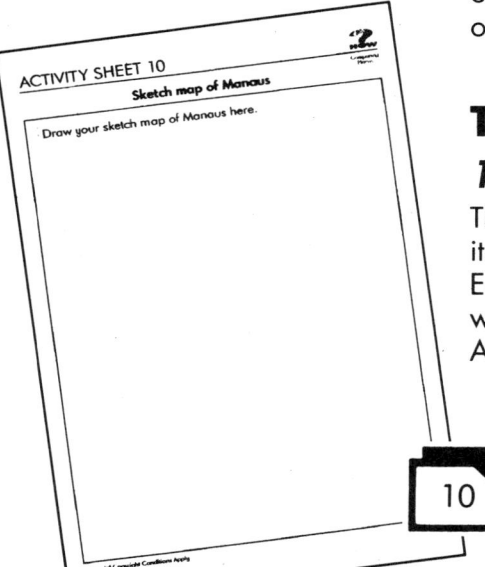

## Teaching and Learning Notes

### 1. Drawing a sketch map of Manaus

The map on page 19 of the textbook shows the port area of Manaus and its main features. Children can list these, matching them with Photos A–D. Encourage them to make their own tourist map of Manaus, selecting which features they want to show. Ask them to explain their choices. Activity Sheet 10: *Sketch map of Manaus* can be used here.

---

*Assessment opportunities*
KEY SoA:    Gg1/4f

*Other SoA which could be assessed:*
        Gg1/3c

*Statements of Attainment*
Draw a sketch map using symbols and a key

Make a map of a short route, showing features in the correct order

Discuss with the children how they could represent features by drawing symbols for them on the sketch map. Talk about the purpose of a key. It will help if you have available a range of maps with keys for them to look at. The children should consider and debate the selection of symbols. How many would they include on a given map and for what reasons? (Too many will clutter the available space on a map.) What are the critical details for the map's specific purpose? (What will the map's audience want to access quickly and easily?)

Unlike Activity Sheet 8, Activity Sheet 10 does not have a box to prompt the children to add a key. The children will need to remember to add their own.

## 2. The region around Manaus

Discuss what kinds of features a tourist might find in the area adjacent to the Amazon, Negro and Solimoes junction. (More information on page 25.) Encourage the children to include these on a sketch map to help tourists to find local features. They could start by making a classification of these – for example, natural scenery, cultural attractions.

# Extensions and Variations

Activity Sheet 11: *Draw a route* provides additional practice in drawing a route. The children should choose a route they know well. For assessment purposes, it will be helpful if it is a route that you are also familiar with. The criterion given is that the route must include going round two corners. Encourage the children to mark as many features as possible on their route.

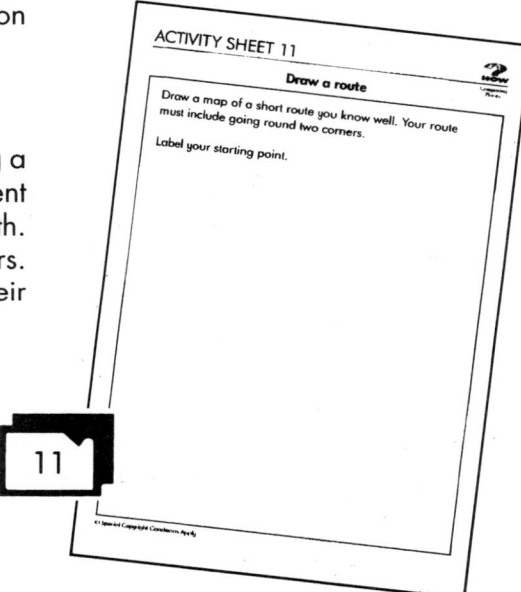

---

| *Evidence of attainment* | *Bases of assessment* |
| --- | --- |
| Child draws sketch map with key to explain the main symbols used on the map | Product |
| Child makes a map of a local route (s)he knows well. The route should include 3 features in correct sequence and at least one change of direction | Product |

# 9: BETWEEN TWO POINTS: BRISTOL

## Learning Opportunities

There are opportunities for children to develop the understanding, skills and attitudes involved in:

▲ using a scale to measure distances accurately on a map

▲ looking for and suggesting reasons why the shortest (straight line) route between places is not always possible

▲ observing features on maps

▲ suggesting why different forms of transport are sometimes used

## Teaching and Learning Notes

### 1. Measuring distances

Measuring the straight-line distance between two points on the Ordnance Survey map of a section of Bristol provides a context for looking at scales and their use in measuring distances between places or points accurately on maps. Here the focus is on measuring the straight-line distance between two fixed points (A and B) on the OS section (Gg1/4b). This is reinforced by measuring the straight-line distance between Hambrook and Stapleton.

### 2. Looking at motorway links

Ask the children to find the junction of the M32 with the M4 (top right-hand corner) and to suggest reasons why the M32 does not follow a straight-line route into Bristol. Careful observation of the map will show that the settlements of Frenchay, Broomhill, Stapleton, etc, would have proved obstacles to such a route. Places like these need to be by-passed when new roads are built. Note also such higher points of ground as Sims' Hill, which roadbuilders would avoid (or tunnel through if detours proved too costly).

### 3. Other forms of transport

The children should look at the map to see what other means of transport are shown. They will find the railway (with mainline stations at Bristol Parkway and Bristol Temple Meads). Some may also notice the harbour, or know about the airport.

| Assessment opportunities | Statements of Attainment |
|---|---|
| KEY SoAs: Gg1/4b | Measure the straight line distance between two points on a plan |
| Gg4/4d | Explain why roads and railways may not always take the shortest route between the places they link |
| *Other SoA which could be assessed:* | |
| Gg4/3c | Explain why different forms of transport are used |

# Extensions and Variations

Discuss with the children the different forms of transport they have used. How many different forms do they use regularly? When is one form of transport better than another? On Activity Sheet 12: *How will they travel?* the children will need to make decisions about the best form of transport in different situations. There are no correct answers, but the children should be able to explain the reasoning behind their choices.

For Gg4/3c (explain why different forms of transport are used) it is important that the child has the opportunity to show (or reveal in response to structured questions about the written response) that s/he understands that the length of the journey, the time available, and the cost (or social circumstances of the traveller) all influence the form of transport used.

| *Evidence of attainment* | *Bases of assessment* |
| --- | --- |
| Child measures distance correctly between A and B *and* Hambrook and Stapleton | Oral/Written |
| Child gives *two* reasons why the M32 does not run in a straight line | Oral/Written |
| Child fills in Activity Sheet 12, giving logical reasons in each case why the form of transport was chosen | Product |

# 10: TRANSPORT TO AND FROM MANAUS

## Learning Opportunities

There are opportunities for children to develop the understanding, skills and attitudes involved in:

▲ exploring reasons for matching transport routes to physical environments

▲ suggesting why roads do not always take the shortest route between places they link

▲ investigating ways in which human actions have changed the landscape

## Background Information

The traditional form of transport in the Amazonia region has been by ship. The rainforest is crisscrossed by rivers and Manaus, although nearly 2,500km from the sea, can be reached by ships of over 10,000 tonnes.

River transport has obvious limitations, and to promote and expedite development, the Brazilian government began building a network of roads. The Transamazonica Highway is a gravel road that crosses the rainforest from east to west for a distance of 6,400km. The enterprise was beset with problems: poor pre-planning and surveying; protests by local Amazon tribes; disease among the constructors; torrential rain and flooding. The gravel surface still develops deep ruts, and abandoned vehicles are an occupational hazard, as are stretches made impassable by mud-laden landslides and river floods.

However the Highway is the focus of a scheme to provide a 'growth corridor' with development planned for strips of land on either side of it and its feeder roads. Although over half a million individual families have settled along the Highway, many left on finding that the land was unsuited for farming. The main beneficiaries have been companies investing in large-scale ranching, lumbering and mining projects in the Amazon basin. The negative effect on the rainforest has been well-documented, and will be discussed in the context of the region's natural resources on pages 38 and 39 of the pupil book.

---

*Assessment opportunities*     *Statements of Attainment*

KEY SoAs:  Gg1/4b            Measure the straight line distance between two points on a plan

Gg4/4d            Explain why roads and railways may not always take the shortest route between the places they link

*Other SoAs which could be assessed:*

Gg2/4b            Describe how the landscape of a locality outside the local area has been changed by human actions

Gg4/5d            Compare road and rail (in this case, river) networks and explain effects of changes to these networks

# Teaching and Learning Notes

## 1. Transport in the Amazon basin

Discuss with the children why a road was not begun in the Amazon area until 1968. Why do they think the inhabitants of the area had been satisfied with only river transport for so long? Look at the route taken by the Transamazonica Highway and compare it with a physical relief map of the region. Discuss why it does not run in the straight line patterns that you see on motorway maps of the UK. (The immense scale of the map of Brazil tends to blur turns in the road caused by the need to avoid the high ground in the south and by the approaches to the many rivers. Unlike the roads in Bristol, the Highway is attracted, rather than repelled, by human settlements. The many tributaries of the Amazon are usually crossed by ferry.) On Activity Sheet 13: *The Transamazonica Highway*, the children can mark the route of the Highway and write suggestions on their map for its meandering route. Encourage them to refer to the key.

## 2. Measuring straight-line distances

The children can practise measuring the straight line distance between various points on the map of the Amazon region on page 23 of the textbook. To give them an idea of the huge distances involved, tell them that the distance from Land's End to John o'Groats is about 1000km – roughly the distance between Manaus and Porto Velho.

## 3. Comparing types of transport

Motorways are frequently used in this country for transporting freight from place to place. Discuss why this is not the case in Brazil. What other ways are there of moving freight around? The children could make a chart showing the benefits and drawbacks of using different types of transport in and around Manaus. For each method of transport, the children could indicate how it could best be used, e.g. planes – for transporting people.

# Extensions and Variations

Talk about how different groups of Brazil's population have been affected by the road construction – rainforest tribes, farmers, road construction workers, business investors in the area, etc. Put together researched statements and hold a group meeting to role play personal positions and opinions *vis à vis* the Highway.

| *Evidence of attainment* | *Bases of assessment* |
|---|---|
| Child correctly measures straight-line distance between Manaus and Santarém *and* Manaus and Porto Velho | Oral/Written |
| Child gives *two* reasons for deviations in the Transamazonica Highway related to the physical environment | Oral/Written |
| Child identifies changes which have occurred to settlements along the Highway, and discusses their effects | Oral/Written |
| Child contrasts and describes recent changes in river and road transport in the Amazon region | Oral |

# 11: MAKING CHANGES: BRISTOL

## Learning Opportunities

There are opportunities for children to develop the understanding, skills and attitudes involved in:

▲ noticing landscape changes

▲ categorizing these changes as made by human actions

▲ investigating changes in landscapes of other localities, and comparing these to the local area

▲ using correct geographical vocabulary

▲ distinguishing between different types of land-use

▲ discussing conflicts that can arise over land-use

## Background Information

Bristol became an important port during the 17th century, largely as a result of its focal position on the infamous 'triangular trade' route between West Africa and the West Indies. Cheap goods were taken to Africa; slaves exchanged for the goods were transported to the West Indies; tobacco, cocoa and other items from the Indies were brought back into Bristol – making huge profits for the merchants over the original cargo of trinkets that had been taken to Africa.

The buildings spread out along the waterfront to make a busy and prosperous centre. Some of these buildings inevitably fell into disuse over time, others survived until they were bombed during the Second World War and redevelopment is changing the use, if not the face, of the remainder.

## Teaching and Learning Notes

### 1. Old buildings, new uses

There are still approximately 60 timber-framed buildings built before 1700 in the centre of Bristol. Discuss with the children what they think happened to the rest.

*Assessment opportunities*

KEY SoA:    Gg2/4b

*Statements of Attainment*

Describe how the landscape of a locality outside the local area has been changed by human actions

*Other SoAs which could be assessed:*

Gg2/3c — Use correct geographical vocabulary to identify types of landscape features and activities with which they are familiar in the local area

Gg2/3d — Compare features and occupations of the local area with the other localities specified in the programme of study

Gg4/3d — Distinguish between those uses of land which require large sites and those which occupy small sites

Gg4/4e — Give reasons for the ways in which land is used, how conflict can arise because of competition over the use of land, and for the location of different types of economic activity

Gg2/3e — Explain the relationships between types of land-use, buildings and human activities in the local area

Talk about the changes of use shown in the photos on the spread. Discuss possible reasons for the changes in each case. Compare these with similar types of changes in your own locality.

## 2. Looking at the local area

This task gives children the opportunity to link what they have learned about Bristol to the local area. The children could make a survey of features in the local area and investigate changes to their use. Each child should pick out one feature they would like to focus on and record their findings on Activity Sheet 14: *Changes to my local area*. Children should be encouraged to use correct geographical vocabulary when discussing features.

# Extensions and Variations

Using the Bristol spreads in the textbook, the children could list all the changes that have been made to the city. How many of these have been made by human actions? How many were likely to have been planned changes? Encourage the children to think of the issues surrounding new developments in the local area. For example, if a leisure centre is being planned, who will benefit from it and why? Why might some people wish the land (and money!) to be used in a different way?

Different activities and features require different amounts of space. Activity Sheet 15: *Which land-use needs more space?* gets the children to explore this issue and to give reasons for their choices between each pair of locations. The single line limits the response, so opportunities should be made to ask the children for the reasons behind their choices.

Activity Sheet 16: *Shops in the local area* will encourage children to think about why local features are situated where they are. Shops need to be accessible to their customers. If the shops marked are corner (or small) shops, then the clientele are likely to to be within walking distance. On the other hand, supermarkets are most usually reached by car or public transport.

---

| *Evidence of attainment* | *Bases of assessment* |
|---|---|
| Child gives *three* indicators of change in Bristol caused by human action and indicates whether these were planned or not | Oral/Written |
| Child correctly names six local types of features using geographical vocabulary | Oral/Written |
| Child compares three local features with those in Bristol, identifying similar or different | Oral/Written |
| Child fills in Activity Sheet 15 and justifies choice made | Oral/Written |
| Child identifies one local issue over how land is used (e.g. a superstore project, multi-storey car park, leisure centre) and links its location to an economic reason (e.g. in the superstore example, potential pool of customers) | Oral/Written |
| Child marks shops on her/his map of the local area (on Activity Sheet 16) and indicates which houses use those shops. Child should discuss advantages and disadvantages of shops' location | Written/Oral |

# 12: CHANGING TIMES: MANAUS

## Learning Opportunities

There are opportunities for children to develop the understanding, skills and attitudes involved in:

▲ identifying uses of natural resources
▲ explaining why different forms of transport are used
▲ identifying and giving reasons for the location of activities in the local area
▲ observing and describing how the landscape of a locality has been changed by human actions
▲ comparing activities and features in Manaus with those in the local area

## Background Information

Brazil, in common with other developing countries, has turned to tourism as a major earner of foreign currency. It attracts tourists from many parts of the world and has a national tourist authority, *Embratur*.

## Teaching and Learning Notes

### 1. Uses of rubber

The task asks the children to make a list of uses for rubber. They will probably come up with some of the following: tyres (all sorts), shoe soles, rubber bands, wellington boots, pencil erasers, rubber gloves and rubber sheets. Investigate and classify the occasions they might use rubber goods and link them to the types they identify. (Just for the record, goods traditionally made of rubber are now more likely to be made from synthetic elastomers – worldwide sales of condoms are now the mainstay of the natural rubber industry!)

| Assessment opportunities | Statements of Attainment |
|---|---|
| KEY SoAs: Gg4/3c | Explain why different forms of transport are used |
| Gg2/4b | Describe how the landscape of a locality outside the local area has been changed by human actions |
| Other SoAs which could be assessed: | |
| Gg2/3d | Compare features and occupations of the local area with the other localities specified in the Programme of Study |
| Gg2/3f | Explain why some activities in the local area are located where they are |
| Gg4/5c | Explain the reasons for the growth of economic activities in particular locations |

## 2. Travelling to Manaus

Explore ways of getting to Manaus. Tourists might arrive by plane or boat, or even by bus. Discuss reasons for using these alternative methods of making journeys (Gg4/3c). Extend the discussion by inviting children to suggest links with the purposes of the tourists' visits to the city and its surroundings. There are direct flights from Brasilia and Rio de Janeiro into Manaus (journey time: 3½ hours). Its airport is one of the main entry points into the country.

## 3. Making a tourist brochure

Use the map on page 27 of the pupil book and investigate other potential sources of information to discover what tourists might wish to see in the region – a large collage day-diary of visits and sights would be one form of record. Find out about the *igarapés* (small creeks) and the wildlife tourists would encounter while on a trip down the river Negro. A day boat trip from Manaus takes the tourists to the 'meeting of the waters' where the black waters of the River Negro meet the brown waters of the River Solimoes, and flow for several miles side by side without mixing. They can swim or even camp in the rainforest overnight.

Food specialities include fish dishes like *tucunare* and *pirarucu* (the latter is the largest freshwater fish in the world). There are over 1500 fish species in the Amazon. Shopping is another tourist attraction in Manaus. In the Free Trade Zone imported goods can be bought free of duty. There are also local Amerindian arts and crafts for sale from all over the region.

Identify changes that are likely to have been made in the landscape of Manaus in the last twenty years, e.g. the airport, building of hotels, restaurants, shops, etc., to attract tourists and to provide for their needs.

## 4. Tourism in your home region

Discuss places or features that attract visitors to your home region (or local area if sufficient material). Talk about why these features are located where they are and investigate reasons if they are not immediately obvious. As far as you can, make comparisons with Manaus.

| Evidence of attainment | Bases of assessment |
| --- | --- |
| Child gives reasons why tourists might use *two* different forms of transport to reach Manaus | Oral |
| Child gives *two* examples of how Manaus' landscape has been changed by human actions to meet the needs of visitors | Written/Oral |
| Child compares three types of local features with those in Manaus, identifying similar or different | Written/Oral |
| Child describes two activities in the local area and explains why they are situated where they are (e.g. a factory needs a lot of room, so it isn't in the centre of town) | Written/Oral |
| Child describes reasons why Manaus has become a centre for tourism | Oral |

# 13: HOW BRISTOL IS CHANGING

## Learning Opportunities

There are opportunities for children to develop the understanding, skills and attitudes involved in:

▲ observing changes in a locality
▲ noting how those changes are the result of human actions
▲ realizing that these changes are planned
▲ drawing a sketch map
▲ using correct geographical vocabulary

## Background Information

See also page 32 for information on Bristol's historical role as a port.

In the last fifty years, the centres of Britain's large cities have largely emptied of people. They have been rehoused either in suburban housing developments built outside the inner city or in surrounding smaller towns; near enough to get into the city for work without using up that valuable land in the centre of the city. (In the city centres, space is at a premium, leading to high cost, rents and rates.)

In cities such as London, Liverpool and Bristol, which have sea-going traditions and whole areas of decaying unused docklands, these dock and warehousing sites are sometimes converted into homes to repopulate the previously unfashionable 'older' districts.

## Teaching and Learning Notes

### 1. Changes to city life

Talk about these changes in the pattern of inner city life. Depending on your local circumstances you may have to use further examples from the cities above or you may have a rich resource on your own doorstep on which to focus discussion, such as: Where have the people gone to? What happened when (large) family groupings were broken up and parts of families moved to different locations? Can they map (illustrate in a sequence of sketches) the changes that took place in their city (or nearest relevant location) over a specified period of time? What does the centre of that place look like now compared to 50 years ago?

Classify the types of building that now occupy land in the centre of a chosen city. Identify and indicate on a plan of the area how much land is occupied (in area and proportionately) by offices, shops, hotels, bus or railway stations, car parking, etc.

---

| Assessment opportunities | Statements of Attainment |
|---|---|
| KEY SoA:   Gg2/4b | Describe how the landscape of a locality outside the local area has been changed by human actions |
| *Other SoAs which could be assessed:* | |
| Gg1/4f | Draw a sketch map using symbols and a key |
| Gg2/3c | Use correct geographical vocabulary to identify types of landscape features and activities with which they are familiar in the local area |

## 2. Looking at plans of Bristol

With the children, look at the plan of Bristol and compare it with the maps of Bristol shown on pages 5 and 9 of the pupil book. How many of the areas named on the plan can they find on the maps? What changes are shown? What are the areas used for now? What thoughts do the children have on the intended action?

## 3. Planning changes

Each child could choose one area of the plan that they would like to change. They could draw plans or sketches of what individual buildings or the whole area would look like using Activity Sheet 17: *Planning for Bristol*. Encourage them to consider how the buildings will be used, and what facilities the people working or shopping in the buildings will need, e.g. parking, disabled access, etc.

## 4. Attracting new businesses

Move on to discuss how new businesses could be attracted to use the shops or offices they have created. The children could work in groups to plan an advertising campaign and design the advertisements.

## Evidence of attainment

Child gives account of *two* changes that have been made to the centre of Bristol

Child shows types of buildings in the city centre on sketch map

Child uses correct geographical vocabulary for six different types of building

## Bases of assessment

Oral/Written

Product

Oral/Written

# 14: THE CHANGING FACE OF MANAUS

## Learning Opportunities

There are opportunities for children to develop the understanding, skills and attitudes involved in:

▲ observing and describing changes made in a landscape by human action

▲ comparing occupations in the local area with those in another locality

▲ considering competition for land-use

## Background Information

More than half the total population of Amazonia lives within the city boundaries of Manaus. This mass of humanity has congregated here from the hinterland and further afield attracted by the prospect of employment in the recent industrial expansion. This includes working on the docks of the freeport, in the new factories of the electronics industry, as well as the hotels and restaurants of the tourist industry (see Section 12).

This massive growth rate was promoted by the government. It created the freeport and improved the port facilities, built the airport, and provided electricity and all the infrastructure needed for modern industrial development.

## Teaching and Learning Notes

### 1. Comparing exports

Talk about the information given on the pie charts about Brazil's industries over the last 70 years. Then focus on the decline of the rubber industry over the same period and discuss possible reasons. Refer the children back to section 12. Where else in the world is there a thriving rubber industry?

---

*Assessment opportunities*  
KEY SoAs: Gg2/4b

*Statements of Attainment*  
Describe how the landscape of a locality outside the local area has been changed by human actions

Gg2/3d

Compare features and occupations of the local area with other localities specified in the Programme of Study

*Other SoAs which could be assessed:*  
Gg4/4e

Give reasons for the ways in which land is used, how conflict can arise because of competition over the use of land, and for the location of different types of economic activity

Gg4/5c

Explain reasons for growth of economic activities in particular locations

## 2. New industries in Manaus

Think about Manaus' location in relation to the rest of Brazil and its other big cities. Discuss why the place might have been chosen as the centre of this industrial 'boom'. Talk about its location on the Amazon, the reasons for the government's desire to develop industry in Amazonia and the availability of a pool of 'cheap labour' in the immediate area.

## 3. What is a freeport?

A freeport (sometimes a free zone within a port), is an area within which all the usual freight handling activities of a port can take place without involving any customs paperwork or charges. The intention is to encourage trade. As soon as the goods are taken out of the area into the country that encloses it, customs become due. Many large European ports have this facility, including Hamburg and Liverpool. Manaus is an example of a freeport within which an area has been set aside as a free zone for industry, in order to promote industrial expansion.

The children may like to do some further research in connection with the 600 acres of active dockland in Liverpool that have been designated a free port zone. This will open up AT2 and AT4 investigations into the reasons why the freeport is not on the site of the original Liverpool docks, and the re-use of that land (for example, the Albert Dock projects, the Maritime Museum, etc.).

# Extensions and Variations

Although the Brazilian rubber industry has now almost completely died out, an investigation of the Malaysian rubber industry could provide an interesting extension.

| Evidence of attainment | Bases of assessment |
|---|---|
| Child names *three* visible changes that have been made to Manaus (e.g. building of airport, port improvements, electronic factories, electric power) | Oral/Written |
| Child compares three local features with those in Manaus, identifying similar or different | Written/Oral |
| Child gives an example of a conflict over the use of land, either from the local area, or relating to Manaus (e.g. rainforests vs new industry) | Written/Oral |
| Child gives 3 reasons for an industrial boom in Manaus | Oral |

# 15: USING LAND IN BRISTOL

## Learning Opportunities

There are opportunities for children to develop the understanding, skills and attitudes involved in:

▲ identifying features on an aerial photo
▲ observing differences between land use on small and large sites
▲ suggesting reasons to distinguish between large and small sites for specific land use
▲ giving reasons for land use in specific locations

## Background Information

Photo A shows a typical mix of land-use around the edge of a big city – fields, farms, houses, and a new motorway interchange. There is no plan to redevelop the area shown in the photograph, as far as we know. The view was simply chosen to illustrate a point, and 'Site A' and 'Site B' were invented for the same purpose.

## Teaching and Learning Notes

### 1. Using Site A

Consider the oblique aerial photo of the outskirts of Bristol. How many features can the children spot? Point out sites A and B. Discuss the amount of land contained by each site. Talk about the land requirements of the items on the list. Encourage the children to bring direct experience to bear wherever possible. Have any of them visited or seen an airport? How big was it? How much land did it cover? Have they ever used a bottle bank? How much land does it cover? Lead towards informed choice of use for site A. The children should use Activity Sheet 18: *Using land* to show their choice and give reasons for it.

| *Assessment opportunities* | *Statements of Attainment* |
|---|---|
| KEY SoA:    Gg4/4e | Give reasons for the ways in which land is used, how conflict can arise because of competition over the use of land, and for the location of different types of economic activity |

*Other SoAs which could be assessed:*

| | |
|---|---|
| Gg1/3d | Identify features on aerial photographs |
| Gg4/3d | Distinguish between those uses of land which require large sites and those which occupy small sites |
| Gg2/3e | Explain the relationships between types of land-use, buildings and human activities in the local area |
| Gg2/3f | Explain why some activities in the local area are located where they are |

## 2. Using Site B

Do a similar exercise with site B as for site A. What clues does the photo give you about the suitability of site B for its use as a farm? Why might the superstore company want the land? Look at its location carefully. What would the superstore be interested in? (people as customers) Are there centres of population nearby? What about transport to the store? Discuss the kinds and number of access routes shown on the photo. Get the children to discuss other factors the company might find to make this an attractive site. Apply to a local example of small-scale land use within larger sites, e.g. location of can banks in school playgrounds.

For Gg/3e children should be given the opportunity to show that they understand that the type of building or other land-use in the local area reflects the activity which takes place there. For evidence of attainment, children should be able to explain the link between three different types of buildings or other land-uses and activities which take place in or on each of these.

## 3. For and against

What might the local feeling be about the change of use? Encourage the children to discuss and list opinions for and against, backing the comments with evidence from the photo where applicable.

| Evidence of attainment | Bases of assessment |
|---|---|
| Child gives *two* reasons for the superstore company wanting to build on the farm site; *and* one local reason *for* and one *against* | Written/Oral |
| Child identifies *three* features from the aerial photo | Oral |
| Child gives a logical choice and reason for the use of sites A *and* B | Written/Oral |
| Child identifies the relationships between three buildings or land-use in the local area and human activities which take place in them | Oral |
| Child explains why some activities in the local area are located where they are | Oral |

## Learning Opportunities

There are opportunities for children to develop the understanding, skills and attitudes involved in:

▲ looking at patterns of settlement

▲ exploring cross-sections of city developments

▲ discussing reasons for land-use zones in a city

▲ drawing a sketch map

▲ distinguishing between those uses of land which require large sites and those which occupy small sites

## Background Information

Until 20-25 years ago the majority of people in economically developing countries tended to live a rural life, earning their living from farming activities. This trend has now been reversed, with people moving to cities, lured by the prospect of work and wages, the keys to a better standard of living.

Brazil is conspicuously affected by this migratory process. Manaus is a typical example of a swollen city's difficulties in sustaining the influx.

In Brazil's cities, the percentage of 'squatters' living in slum-like settlements is steadily increasing. In Brasilia and Recife the 'people of the *favelas*' make up over 60 per cent of the population, while in Rio de Janeiro and São Paulo the proportion is 40 per cent and increasing rapidly.

## Teaching and Learning Notes

### 1. Cross-section of a typical Brazilian city

The cross-section on page 34 of the pupil book shows the clear demarcation lines that exist between the sectors. The old tenements with poor quality of housing with basic amenities at least has a permanence which the *favelas* are denied. Usually these are basic squatter settlements with the homes being constructed from rubbish – cardboard, corrugated sheets, old tyres – and lacking even the most basic services and sanitation. In Manaus the 'favelas' tend to be constructed along the *igarapés* or creeks which cut into the city from the river. Land here is cheap – rather, unwanted – because the river can rise as much as 14 metres in the winter rains, so permanent buildings will be destroyed. Temporary buildings, of course, can be rebuilt.

---

*Assessment opportunities*

KEY SoA:    Gg4/4e

*Statements of Attainment*

Give reasons for the ways in which land is used, how conflict can arise because of competition over the use of land, and for the location of different types of economic activity

*Other SoAs which could be assessed:*

Gg4/3d

Distinguish between those uses of land which require large sites and those which occupy small sites

Gg1/4f

Draw a sketch map using symbols and a key

---

Talk to the children about why people have left the Brazilian countryside to live in the *favelas*. Are there any advantages in such a move? Describe a *favela* dweller's walk through the city as shown on the cross-section. Where would (s)he hope to be located eventually?

## 2. Cross-section of a British city

Discuss with the class how a cross-section of a British city might look. You may be able to obtain a zoning map from your local council. How does the cross section compare with the Brazilian city? The children should draw their cross-section on Activity Sheet 19: *Draw a cross-section*. They could focus on either Bristol, a nearby city with which they are familiar, or another one they have studied.

Discuss with the children which zones will need to be the largest. Why is this?

## 3. What's most expensive?

Discuss with the children why some land-use zones might be more expensive than others. What factors would affect the cost of land? The children should try to decide which zone of the Brazilian city they think will be the the most expensive. Ask them to explain their choice.

# Extensions and Variations

Find out more information on the *favelas* so that you can produce with your group a script for a television documentary about life in a Brazilian *favela*. There are positive aspects: the informality and friendliness of life that depend on the co-operation of neighbours in these extended family situations, the evidence of ingenious use of other people's rubbish (we might call it recycling!). A historical point can be made here, in that the *favelas* of 20th century Brazil are constructed under very similar conditions as the 19th century slums of Britain's industrial revolution. Raise issues such as: What can the city authorities do about the settlements? How can the *favela* inhabitants help themselves further? Does the outside world have a contribution to make?

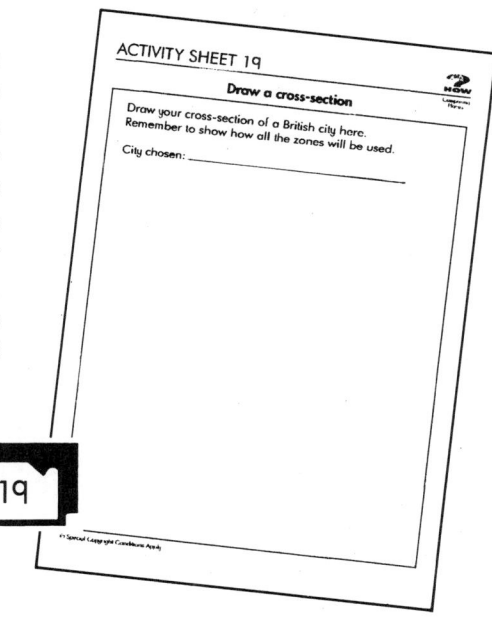

| Evidence of attainment | Bases of assessment |
|---|---|
| Child gives reasons for the land-use in *two* of the zones on the Manaus cross-section | Oral/Written |
| Child explains the reasons behind drawing some of the zones larger than others in the city focus on Activity Sheet 19 | Product/Oral |
| Child draws sketch map showing cross-section of a city. Symbols and a key should be used to show the different zones | Product |

# 17: NATURAL RESOURCES: BRISTOL

## Learning Opportunities

There are opportunities for children to develop the understanding, skills and attitudes involved in:

▲ using correct geographical vocabulary to discuss the range of natural resources which can be obtained from the environment

▲ identifying which natural resources are obtained in their local area or region

▲ identifying the processes for the extraction of these resources

▲ observing how these extraction processes can change environments

▲ designing activities to improve the environment

▲ classifying renewable and non-renewable resources

## Background Information

This section provides opportunities to recap on earlier work on how people obtain materials from the environment (Gg5/2a) and ways in which people have changed their environment (Gg5/2b). This should lead into consideration of the way in which the extraction of certain natural resources can change the appearance of places.

## Teaching and Learning Notes

### 1. Canon's Marsh

Gas was first produced on the Canon's Marsh gasworks site in the 1820s. The position of the site close to the dock meant that coal transported by ship from Wales could be burned without incurring the cost of further travel. The site declined in importance when coal was brought in by rail. Now, gas is no longer manufactured from coal, but piped in from the North Sea, and the site is derelict.

Discuss with the children what kind of development might be being planned for the site of the former gasworks to provide more jobs. Encourage the children to make and annotate a diagram to amplify these suggestions.

| Assessment opportunities | Statements of Attainment |
|---|---|
| KEY SoAs: Gg5/3b | Describe an activity designed to improve the local environment or a place they have visited |
| Gg5/3a | Describe the effects on environments of extracting natural resources |
| Other SoAs which could be assessed: | |
| Gg4/4e | Give reasons for the ways in which land is used, how conflict can arise because of competition over the use of land, and for the location of different types of economic activity |
| Gg2/3f | Explain why some activities in the local area are located where they are |
| Gg5/5b | Distinguish between renewable and non-renewable resources |

## 2. Natural resources

Find out, through discussion, what the children understand by the term 'natural resources'. Let them share ideas and compile a list of natural resources on Activity Sheet 20: *Natural resources.*

Ask the children to note on their list which of the resources are available in your local area. (Depending on your circumstances you may wish to extend this area of study to your region. For the purposes of this exercise you can either decide a suitable extent, or use the standard geographical regional definitions, e.g. north-west England, South-east England, mid-Wales etc.)

## 3. Natural resources in the local area

Discuss the notion of 'extracting' resources and demonstrate how these definitions include the processes required in getting resources to a finished product stage. Talk about the processes by which the local or regional resources that the children have identified are extracted. Get children to access as much information as they can about one of these processes and to make a simple sequence in words or diagram form to show the process from extraction of the resource to its finished product.

Discuss whether the extraction of natural resources has made their area look better or worse or has had no effect. Are there unsightly quarries, mine spoils or slag heaps? Apart from the visible effects, talk about the cumulative longer term effects on the land, sea etc. of continually 'taking' or using these natural resources. Distinguish between renewable and non-renewable resources.

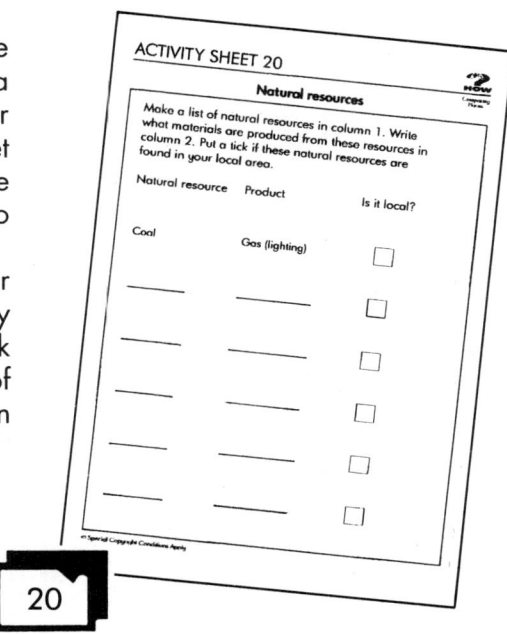

| Evidence of attainment | Bases of assessment |
|---|---|
| Child describes how the derelict site in Bristol could be developed | Written/Oral |
| Child lists three effects on an area of the extraction of natural resources | Written/Oral |
| Child suggests two alternative ways in which the Canon's Marsh site could be used and discusses the pros and cons of each | Oral/Written |
| Child discusses why a local (or regional) site for the extraction of a natural resource is situated where it is | Oral/Written |
| Child classifies and defines 3 renewable and 3 non-renewable resources | Oral/Written |

# 18: VANISHING FOREST: MANAUS

## Learning Opportunities

There are opportunities for children to develop the understanding, skills and attitudes involved in:

▲ learning that a range of natural resources can be obtained from the environment

▲ identifying the processes for the extraction of these resources

▲ observing how these extraction processes can change environments

▲ realizing that some environments need special protection

▲ using an atlas and other reference books to obtain information

▲ classifying renewable and non-renewable resources

## Background Information

The majority of the Amazon basin is less than 200 metres above sea level. It is covered in tropical rainforest. The constant conditions which have sustained rainforest growth can be summarized simply by stating Manaus' climate figures in a typical year: a temperature which never drops below 25°C and is usually nearer 30°C; rainfall which, in the rainy season (December-May) is often over 200mm per month and never below 50mm per month, making the region the wettest in the world. These forests contain thousands or different species of plants (many unknown to the rest of the world) and animals, as well as many indigenous tribes of Amazonian Indians. The patterns of life of these tribes have evolved around the forest's life cycle and they have traditionally used the forest plants as sources of food and medicine.

With the increasing colonization of the rainforest region, its habitat has been (and continues to be) damaged, largely through deforestation, but also by destruction of the ecosystem of the area. By 1990 18 per cent of the rainforest had been cleared for agricultural and industrial schemes, and communication network construction. Road construction in Amazonia (beginning with the Transamazonica Highway, see Section 10) has further opened up areas of rainforest and threatened the life support systems of the indigenous Indians.

Natural resources such as gold, diamonds, bauxite, manganese (Brazil produces 13 per cent of the world's supply), iron, copper, lead and tin are mined in the region. The effects of poorly supervised mining operations have included the destruction of huge tracts of rainforest, pollution of rivers (by oil or petrol from pumping machines, human

| Assessment opportunities | Statements of Attainment |
|---|---|
| KEY SoAs: Gg5/3a | Describe the effects on environments of extracting natural resources |
| Gg5/4b | Discuss whether some types of environment need special protection |
| Other SoAs which could be assessed: | |
| Gg1/4e | Use the index and contents pages to find information in an atlas |
| Gg5/5b | Distinguish between renewable and non-renewable resources |

sewage and highly poisonous mercury scattered by gold prospectors), and the destruction of the homelands and culture of many thousands of Indians.

In one project alone (the Greater Carajas Program), involving the largest iron ore mining development in the world, over 900,000 square km of forest is being destroyed. (The total area of the UK is 244,000 sq. km.)

## Teaching and Learning Notes

### 1. Types of rainforest hardwood

Among the four hundred types of commercially useful hardwood to be found in the Amazonian rainforest (*selva*) are mahogany and teak. Large trees take over a hundred years to reach full size, so regeneration is a very slow process. In south Brazil, there are forests of softwood trees, especially the Parana pine.

### 2 and 3. The effects of deforestation

The children will need to refer to reference books to answer this question. Some books are suggested on page 80. Additional information on the climate of the Amazonia region can be obtained from an atlas, giving children opportunities to practise their indexing skills.

Talk about the negative points of the mineral exploitation and development projects for Amazonia. Try to balance as many of these negative points with positive ones for the future of the region as you can, for example, plans to protect the environment, landscaping, workers for environmental protection, international pressure from environmental groups on multinational companies and their bankers.

## Extensions and Variations

Research further into the lives and cultures of the indigenous Indian peoples. What can be done to help them? One suggestion is the establishment of areas of non-development land. Discuss the pros and cons of such 'reserves' with the children.

Discuss with the children whether resources are renewable or not. What happens to resources when they are over-used? Lead on to discuss whether some environments need special protection. After discussion, the children could fill in Activity Sheet 21: *Damaged environments*.

**21**

ACTIVITY SHEET 21
**Damaged environments**
Tick whether the resource is renewable or non-renewable. Say what will happen if each one is over-used.

|  | Renewable | Non-renewable | Over-used |
|---|---|---|---|
| Fish | ☐ | ☐ | _____ |
| Trees | ☐ | ☐ | _____ |
| Rocks | ☐ | ☐ | _____ |
| Coal | ☐ | ☐ | _____ |
| Oil | ☐ | ☐ | _____ |
| Sheep | ☐ | ☐ | _____ |

| *Evidence of attainment* | *Bases of assessment* |
|---|---|
| Child lists *three* effects on an area of rainforest of extracting materials | Written/Oral |
| Child gives *two* reasons why the Amazon rainforest needs special protection | Written/Oral |
| Child makes use of index and contents page in an atlas to access information about the climate of Amazonia | Observation |
| Child classifies and defines 3 renewable and 3 non-renewable resources | Written/Oral |

# 19: WATER SUPPLY: BRISTOL

## Learning Opportunities

There are opportunities for children to develop the understanding, skills and attitudes involved in:

▲ identifying the main sources of clean water

▲ identifying ways of ensuring a reliable supply of clean water

▲ comparing the water supply for the local area with that for Bristol

## Background Information

In the United Kingdom we expect a supply of water to be readily available whenever we turn on a tap. We also expect that this water is fresh, clean and largely clear of bacterial impurities. There are established mechanisms for filtration and treatment of water in all regions before it is piped to homes. Check the names of the various regional water authorities; they should be able to supply details of their purification and supply procedures.

However, it is worth discussing possible reasons and situations in which water might be polluted, even if only temporarily. Have there been any occasions locally? Issues such as factory waste polluting rivers and canals, fears of nuclear contamination in the Irish Sea, sewage controls, etc., might have local relevance. Discuss possible causes of water shortage in the United Kingdom.

## Teaching and Learning Notes

### 1. Bristol's water supply

With the children, look closely at the diagram of the water supply system shown on page 40 of the pupil book. Discuss where Bristol's water supply comes from. What strategies could be employed if there are shortages for one reason or another? The children should draw their own annotated diagram on Activity Sheet 22: *Bristol's water supply*. If you live in the area shown on the map, look to see where your water supply comes from. How does it compare in distance of line of supply with Bristol's?

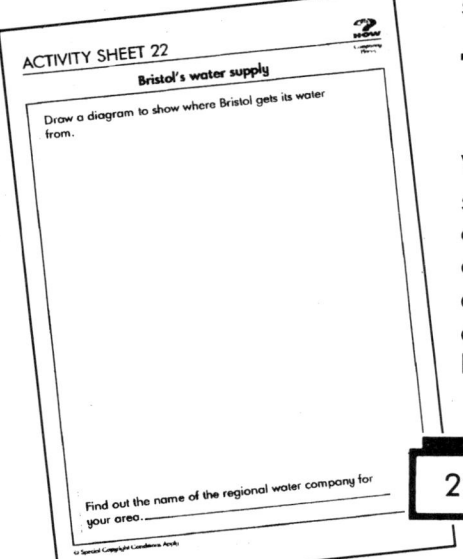

ACTIVITY SHEET 22

Bristol's water supply

Draw a diagram to show where Bristol gets its water from.

Find out the name of the regional water company for your area.

22

---

*Assessment opportunities*

KEY SoA:    Gg5/4a

*Other SoA which could be assessed:*

Gg2/3d

*Statements of Attainment*

Identify the main sources of clean water, and describe ways of ensuring a reliable supply

Compare features and occupations of the local area with the other localities specified in the programme of study

## 2.  Protecting against droughts

Recent dry summers will have raised children's awareness of the potential problems of drought, although these are small compared to those in parts of Africa. In this country the implications of stand pipes, reduced water pressure in domestic appliances at peak times, hose pipe bans on garden watering, etc., could all provide talking points. This can be extended into a comparative study of a more distant place where drought is a real, everyday, life-threatening issue.

## 3.  How water is purified

The children will need to use reference books to answer this question. Some books are suggested on page 80. The class could also write a letter to your local Regional Water Company requesting more information. Discuss with the children the importance for our health of drinking clean water.

---

| *Evidence of attainment* | *Bases of assessment* |
|---|---|
| Child lists *two* sources of clean water *and* describes *one* way of maintaining supply | Written/Oral |
| Child identifies source(s) of water supply for Bristol and compares with their local water supply | Oral |

# 20: WATER SUPPLY: MANAUS

## Learning Opportunities

There are opportunities for children to develop the understanding, skills and attitudes involved in:
▲  investigating water supply to homes in the region
▲  identifying the main sources of clean water
▲  describing ways of ensuring a reliable supply
▲  comparing the water supply for the local area with that in Manaus

## Background Information

Many Brazilians do not have access to clean water supplies, unlike the situation in the United Kingdom where provision of a reliable supply of clean water 'on tap' is taken for granted.

The wealthier and middle income sectors of the Brazilian population usually live in modern houses or apartments in the cities, where water is supplied for bathrooms, washing machines, etc. much as in Britain. However, the poor inhabitants of the recently established *favelas* are unlikely to have piped water or drainage supplied. Often there are open drains breeding disease. Many of the 'homes' in the *favelas* have been built from discarded timber, iron or plastic sheeting, cardboard, anything that will form a shelter. A typical case study of a slum on the outskirts of a Brazilian industrial development described how 'it experiences severe and frequent flooding when the open sewers overflow into the muddy streets. The local rivers are laced with toxic waste, detergents and other industrial pollutants.'

## Teaching and Learning Notes

### 1.  Lack of clean water

Talk about the likely results of lack of clean water in the *favelas*.

To focus the discussion encourage the children to think about how much water they use when they wash their hands, flush the toilet, bath, etc. If water was not instantly available, how would they manage? Talk about other regular uses of water in domestic life, such as washing clothes, cooking, making drinks, cleaning. Talk about the lengthy process the *favela* dweller has to go through to get water from a creek or standpoint and then to ensure it is purified.

| Assessment opportunities | Statements of Attainment |
|---|---|
| KEY SoA:    Gg5/4a | Identify the main sources of clean water, and describe ways of ensuring a reliable supply |
| Other SoA which could be assessed:<br>        Gg2/3d | Compare features and occupations of the local area with the other localities specified in the Programme of Study |

## 2. Water shortages

Try to bring in the children's personal experience as much as possible. For example, has anyone's home ever been short of water or has the water ever been discoloured? What did the family do? What arrangements did they have to make?

If no-one in the class has experienced a water shortage, consider inviting an older member of the community who has, to come in and talk to the class.

## 3. Clean water for favela dwellers

Discuss what Brazilian authorities could do to arrange water supply for the *favela* dwellers, or otherwise alleviate their living conditions.

# Extensions and Variations

What other parts of the world are likely to experience water supply shortages? (An atlas will help the children identify areas of high temperature and low rainfall. Scanning the media will also reveal focus points, both long- and short-term.) How have people in these countries adapted their lifestyles (clothes, buildings, patterns of work, travel and sleep); and their agriculture (crops, irrigation schemes, nomadic farming, etc.) to come to terms with the situation?

Here are some figures for the children to think about (courtesy of WaterAid, address on page 80):

– The average daily consumption in economically developing countries is 10 litres a day. (The World Health Organization regards 20 litres per person per day as the minimum necessary for good health.)

– The average daily consumption in the UK is 150 litres per person per day. Consumption is as follows:
3% is used for drinking
33% is used for cooking and cleaning and is wasted through leaks
32% is used to flush toilets
17% is used in baths and showers
12% is used in washing machines
3% goes on watering the garden and washing the car

Do we use too much? What would be the point of using less?

| Evidence of attainment | Bases of assessment |
| --- | --- |
| Child gives *two* suggestions for providing a clean water supply to the *favelas* | Written/Oral |
| Child makes three comparisons between water supply systems in the local area and those in Manaus | Written/Oral |

# 21: COMPARING BRISTOL AND MANAUS

## Learning Opportunities

There are opportunities for children to develop the understanding, skills and attitudes involved in:

▲ using correct geographical vocabulary to describe features and activities of the local area

▲ identifying features and activities of another locality

▲ comparing features and activities of the local area with those of Bristol and Manaus

▲ using an atlas and other reference books to obtain information

▲ locating features in the local area on a large-scale map

▲ describing how the landscape of Brazil has changed as a result of human actions

## Background Information

This is an opportunity to develop a three-way comparison exercise. Start with an identification of features and activities in the local area (within a 10 minute walk of the school) and then compare these with the identified features of either Bristol or Manaus or both. At this level of investigation, children should be encouraged to classify different types of shops, such as: newsagent, chemist, florist, etc.

## Teaching and Learning Notes

### 1. Comparing Places

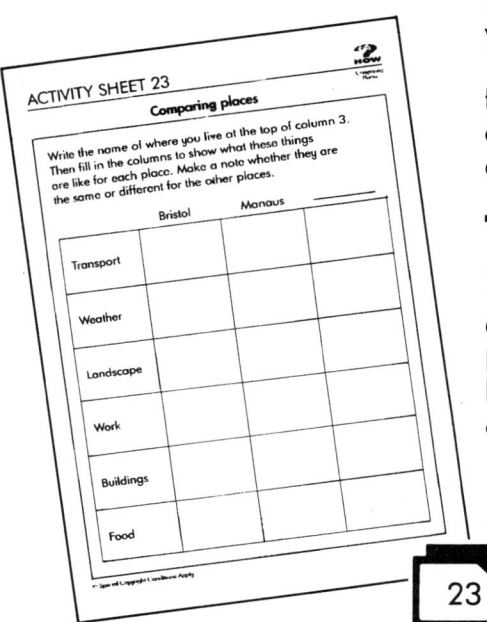

On Activity Sheet 23: *Comparing places*, the children need to compare Bristol and Manaus with regard to transport, weather, landscape, work, buildings and food. The third column on the sheet allows for a three-way comparison with the local area and provides a link with Question 2.

| *Assessment opportunities* | *Statements of Attainment* |
|---|---|
| KEY SoAs: Gg2/3c | Use correct geographical vocabulary to identify types of landscape features and activities with which they are familiar in the local area |
| Gg2/3d | Compare features and occupations of the local area with the other localities specified in the Programme of Study |
| *Other SoAs which could be assessed:* | |
| Gg2/4b | Describe how the landscape of a locality outside the local area has been changed by human actions |
| Gg1/4e | Use the index and contents pages to find information in an atlas |
| Gg1/3b | Use a large-scale map to locate their own position and features outside the classroom |

## 2. Compare and contrast

The children should compare and contrast your local area with either Manaus or Bristol. Encourage the children to use all the spreads in the book as well as other reference books when making their comparisons (see list of books on page 80).

## 3. Make a booklet

Extend the activity to compare features and activities of Brazil with those of the United Kingdom. The maps on page 45 of the pupil book provide a good starting point. This activity will also be enhanced by research in reference books. Activity Sheet 24: *Facts about Brazil* provides a starting point.

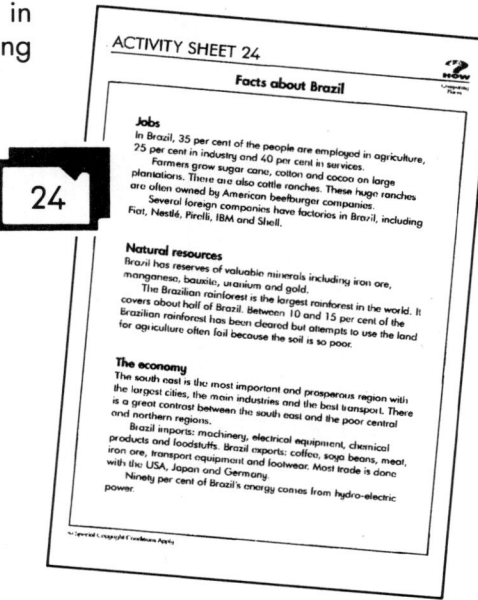

---

| *Evidence of attainment* | *Bases of assessment* |
|---|---|
| Child names *six* features or activities within their local area, using correct geographical vocabulary | Written/Oral |
| Child compares *three* features of the local area with three in Bristol and in Manaus identifying whether similar or different | Written |
| Child includes in brochure details of how the Brazilian landscape has been changed by human actions | Written |
| Child uses index and contents pages to find a range of information in an atlas | Observation/Oral |
| Child locates school and two other features on large-scale map of the local area | Observation |

# ACTIVITY SHEET 1

## Ordnance Survey map of Bristol

The Floating Harbour has co-ordinates

_____ .

Windmill Hill has co-ordinates

_____ .

Hanham Green has co-ordinates

_____ .

Filwood Park has co-ordinates

_____ .

What feature can be found at co-ordinates 6169?

_____ .

There are schools at co-ordinates _____ , _____ and _____ .

Name two features found at co-ordinates 6270.

_____ .

# ACTIVITY SHEET 2

## Map of the United Kingdom

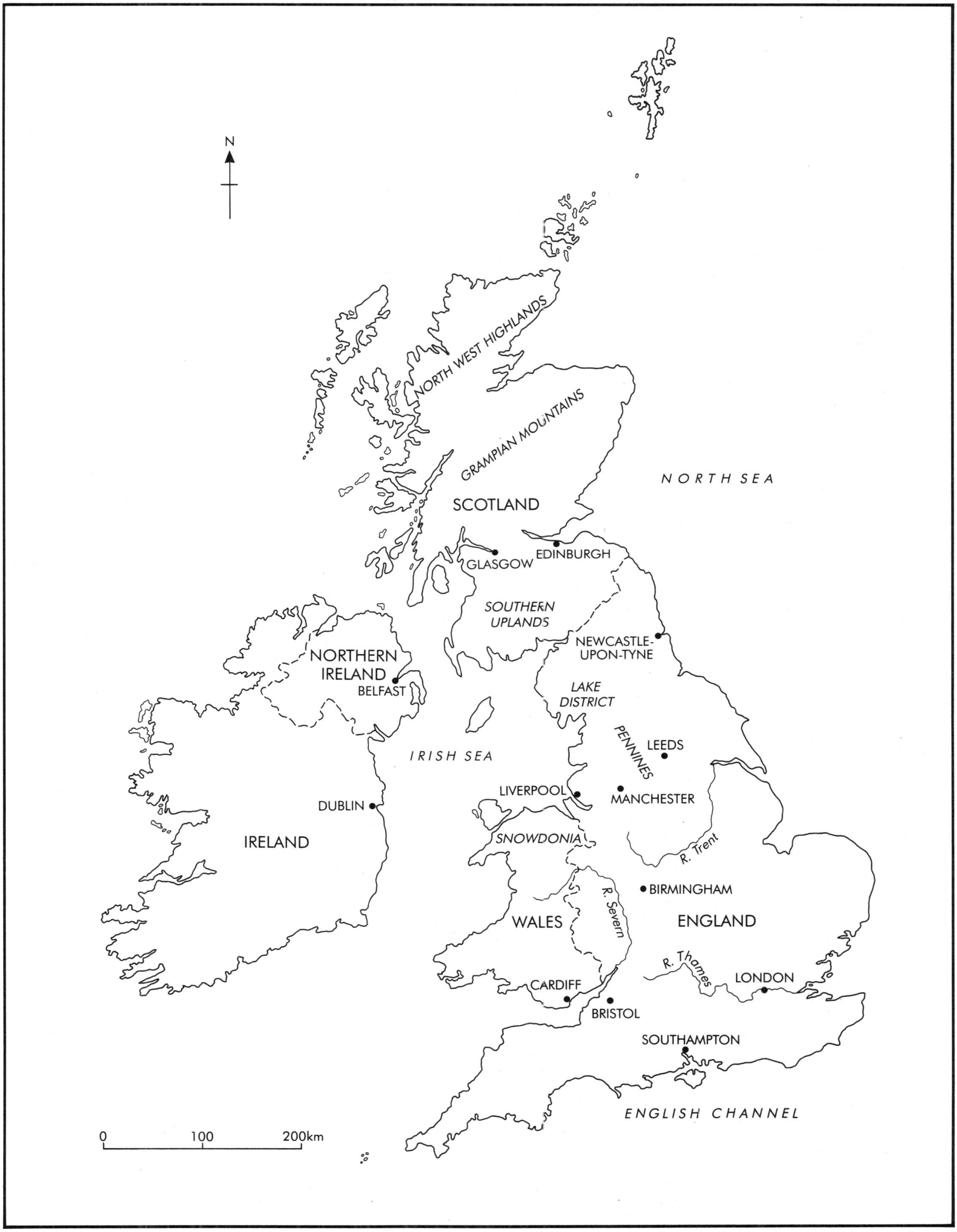

N

NORTH WEST HIGHLANDS

GRAMPIAN MOUNTAINS

*NORTH SEA*

SCOTLAND

GLASGOW ● EDINBURGH

*SOUTHERN
UPLANDS*

NEWCASTLE-
UPON-TYNE ●

NORTHERN
IRELAND

BELFAST ●

*LAKE
DISTRICT*

*IRISH SEA*

PENNINES

LEEDS ●

LIVERPOOL ●

● MANCHESTER

DUBLIN ●

*SNOWDONIA*

*R. Trent*

IRELAND

*R. Severn*

● BIRMINGHAM

WALES

ENGLAND

*R. Thames*

CARDIFF ●

LONDON ●

● BRISTOL

SOUTHAMPTON ●

*ENGLISH CHANNEL*

0        100        200km

# ACTIVITY SHEET 3

## Map of the world

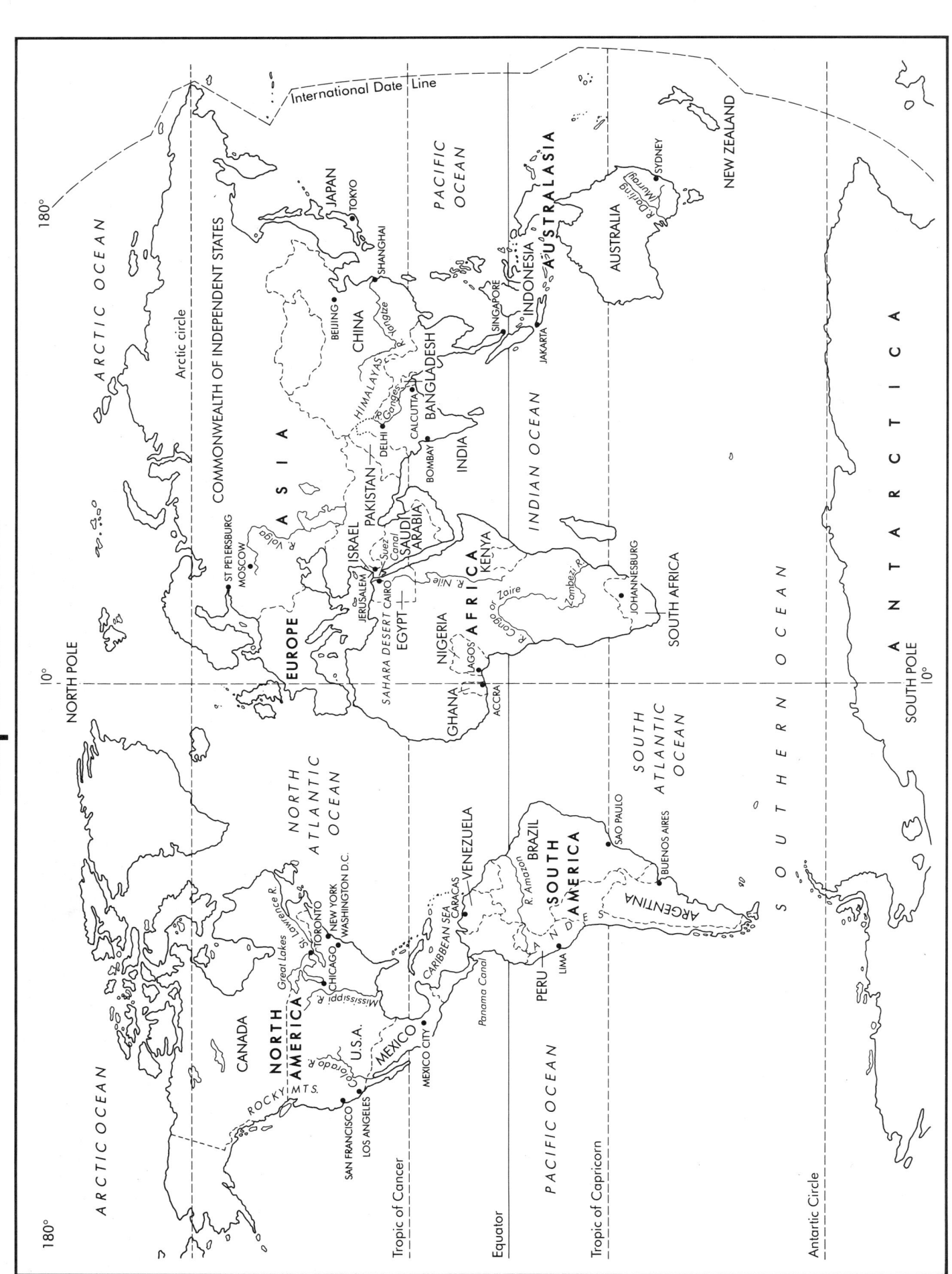

# ACTIVITY SHEET 4

## Identify the features

List five features you can see on both the photo and the map of Bristol on page 9.

Put the numbers in the correct place on the photo.

1 =                    2 =                    3 =

4 =                    5 =

# ACTIVITY SHEET 5

## Why are they there?

Draw two features in your local area.
Give a reason why each is there.

Reason _____

Reason _____

# ACTIVITY SHEET 6

## Features in Manaus

Mark where you can find the following features on the aerial photo of Manaus.

*The Floating Docks*
*The Cathedral*
*The Opera House (Teatro Amazonas)*
*The Customs offices*

# ACTIVITY SHEET 7

## Letter/number coordinates

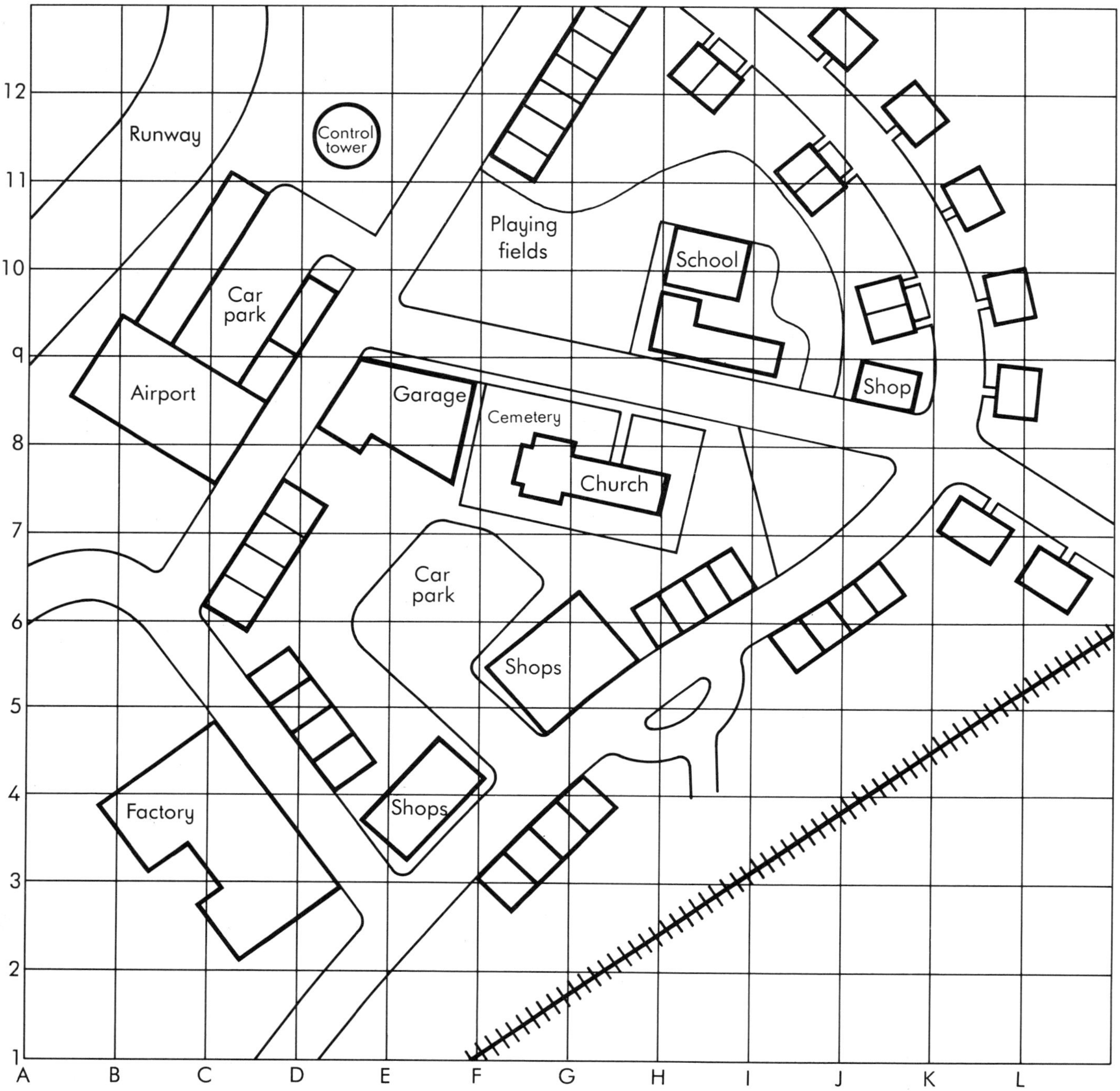

12 — Runway    Control tower

11 — Car park    Playing fields    School

10 — Airport

9 — Garage    Shop

8 — Cemetery    Church

7 — Car park

6 — Shops

5 —

4 — Factory    Shops

3 —

2 —

1 —

A   B   C   D   E   F   G   H   I   J   K   L

In which square is the control tower?_____

In which square is the factory?_____

Mark a station in H3.

# ACTIVITY SHEET 8

## Sketch map of Bristol

Draw a sketch map of Bristol here. Don't forget to
make up symbols to show the features on the map.
Draw a key to show what the symbols mean.

Key

## Features in the local area

Draw and name two features and two activities from your local area.

## Sketch map of Manaus

Draw your sketch map of Manaus here.

# ACTIVITY SHEET 11

## Draw a route

Draw a map of a short route you know well. Your route must include going round two corners.

Label your starting point.

# ACTIVITY SHEET 12

## How will they travel?

Link each person to the best form of transport and say
why you have made your choice.

Why this form
of transport?

_____

_____

_____

John is going
to school.

_____

_____

_____

Pauline is moving
to live in London.

Lewis is going on
holiday to Spain.

_____

_____

_____

Yolanda is going
out to buy clothes.

_____

_____

_____

# ACTIVITY SHEET 13

## The Transamazonica Highway

Mark the route of the Transamazonica Highway on the map.

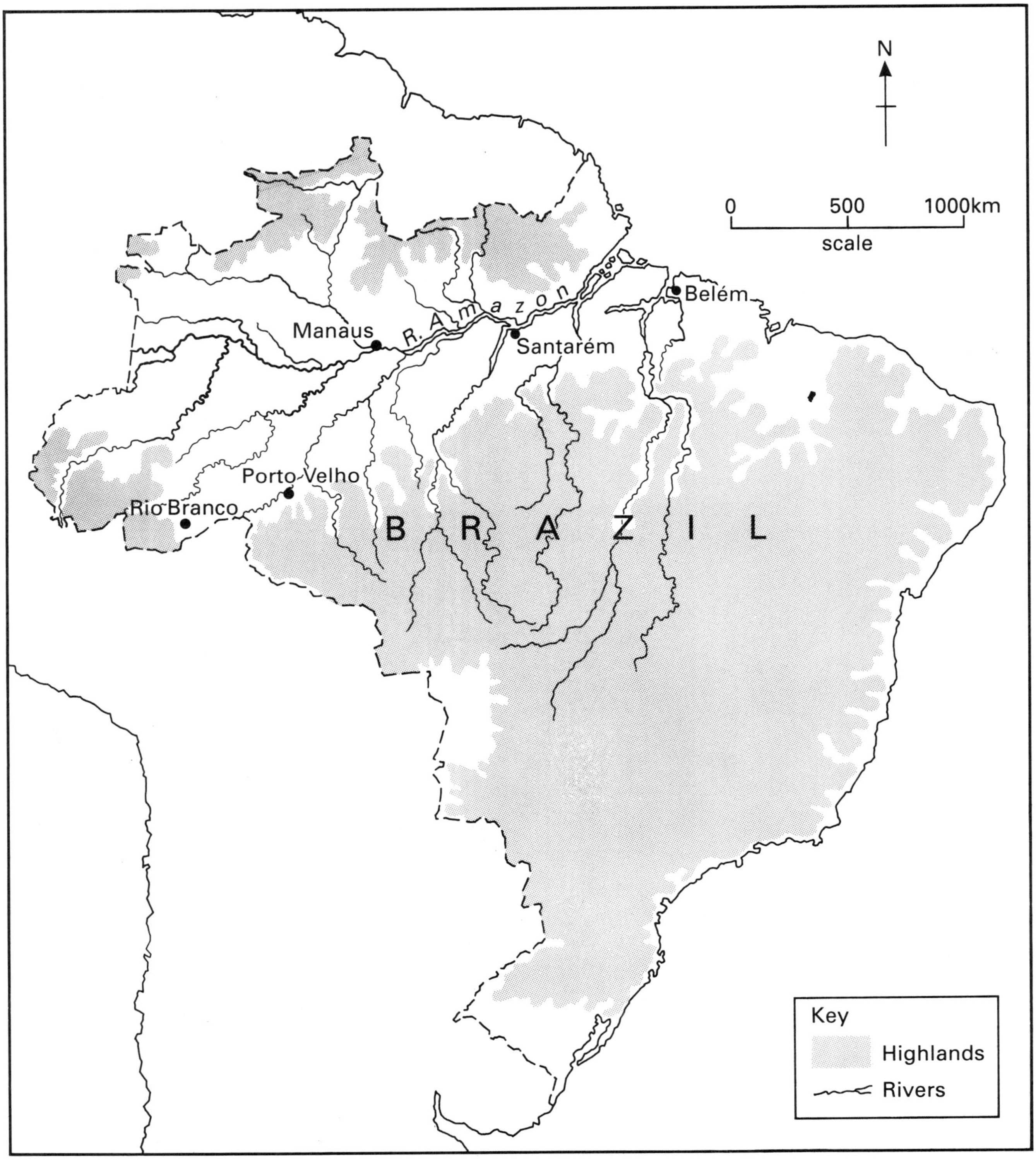

N

| 0 | 500 | 1000km |
scale

Belém

Manaus
R. Amazon
Santarém

Porto Velho

Rio Branco

B R A Z I L

**Key**

Highlands

Rivers

Write reasons on the map for why the Highway does
not follow a straight route.

# ACTIVITY SHEET 14

## Changes to my local area

Draw a place or feature in your local area which has changed its use.

It used to be a _____.

Now it is _____.

## Which land-use needs more space?

Tick the correct box and give a reason.

Reason_____

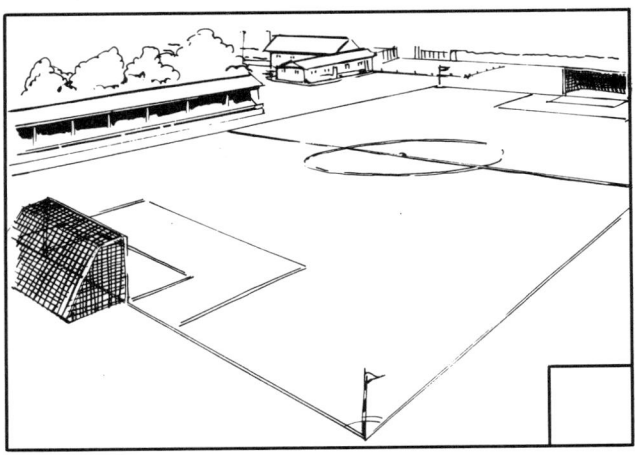

Reason_____

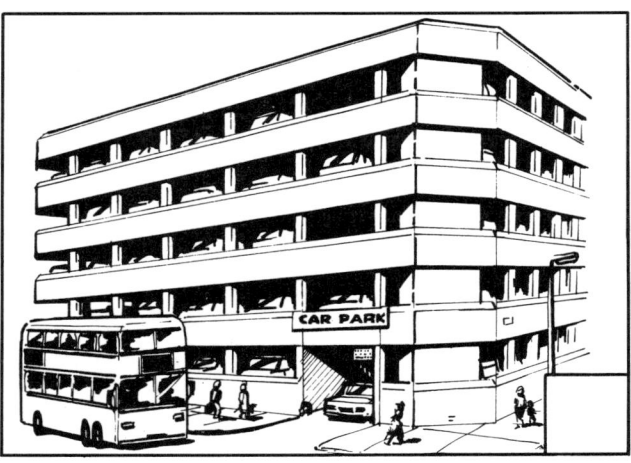

Reason_____

## Shops in the local area

Draw a map of your local area. Mark the shops nearest to where you live. Mark all the houses that use those shops.

## Planning for Bristol

Choose an area (or a building) of Bristol which you feel needs changing. Draw a picture to show what it will look like after your redevelopment has taken place.

# ACTIVITY SHEET 18

## Using land

How do you think Site A should be used?

Car park ☐

Sports field ☐

Bottle bank ☐

School ☐

Superstore ☐

Airport ☐

Reasons for choice: _____

_____

_____

## Draw a cross-section

Draw your cross-section of a British city here.
Remember to show how all the zones will be used.

City chosen: _____

## Natural resources

Make a list of natural resources in column 1. Write what materials are produced from these resources in column 2. Put a tick if these natural resources are found in your local area.

| Natural resource | Product | Is it local? |
| --- | --- | --- |
| Coal | Gas (lighting) | ☐ |
| _____ | _____ | ☐ |
| _____ | _____ | ☐ |
| _____ | _____ | ☐ |
| _____ | _____ | ☐ |
| _____ | _____ | ☐ |

# ACTIVITY SHEET 21

## Damaged environments

Tick whether the resource is renewable or non-renewable. Say what will happen if each one is over-used.

|  | Renewable | Non-renewable | Over-used |
|---|---|---|---|
| Fish | ☐ | ☐ | _____ |
| Trees | ☐ | ☐ | _____ |
| Rocks | ☐ | ☐ | _____ |
| Coal | ☐ | ☐ | _____ |
| Oil | ☐ | ☐ | _____ |
| Sheep | ☐ | ☐ | _____ |

## Bristol's water supply

Draw a diagram to show where Bristol gets its water from.

Find out the name of the regional water company for your area. _____

# ACTIVITY SHEET 23

## Comparing places

Write the name of where you live at the top of column 3. Then fill in the columns to show what these things are like for each place. Make a note whether they are the same or different for the other places.

|  | Bristol | Manaus | _____ |
|---|---|---|---|
| Transport |  |  |  |
| Weather |  |  |  |
| Landscape |  |  |  |
| Work |  |  |  |
| Buildings |  |  |  |
| Food |  |  |  |

## Facts about Brazil

### Jobs

In Brazil, 35 per cent of the people are employed in agriculture, 25 per cent in industry and 40 per cent in services.

Farmers grow sugar cane, cotton and cocoa on large plantations. There are also cattle ranches. These huge ranches are often owned by American beefburger companies.

Several foreign companies have factories in Brazil, including Fiat, Nestlé, Pirelli, IBM and Shell.

### Natural resources

Brazil has reserves of valuable minerals including iron ore, manganese, bauxite, uranium and gold.

The Brazilian rainforest is the largest rainforest in the world. It covers about half of Brazil. Between 10 and 15 per cent of the Brazilian rainforest has been cleared but attempts to use the land for agriculture often fail because the soil is so poor.

### The economy

The south east is the most important and prosperous region with the largest cities, the main industries and the best transport. There is a great contrast between the south east and the poor central and northern regions.

Brazil imports: machinery, electrical equipment, chemical products and foodstuffs. Brazil exports: coffee, soya beans, meat, iron ore, transport equipment and footwear. Most trade is done with the USA, Japan and Germany.

Ninety per cent of Brazil's energy comes from hydro-electric power.

# Record Keeping Chart

| Statement of Attainment | AT1 | | | | | | | | | | | | | | | AT2 | | | | | | | | | | |
|---|---|---|---|---|---|---|---|---|---|---|---|---|---|---|---|---|---|---|---|---|---|---|---|---|---|---|
| | 3a | 3b | 3c | 3d | 4a | 4b | 4c | 4d | 4e | 4f | 5a | 5b | 5c | 5d | 5e | 3a | 3b | 3c | 3d | 3e | 3f | 4a | 4b | 5a | 5b | 5c |
| Sections in which it can be assessed | 5 | 21 | 1 7 8 | 15 | 1 2 | 9 10 | 3 4 | | 5 6 18 21 | 3 7 8 13 16 | | | 1 | | | 6 | | 7 11 13 21 | 4 11 12 14 19 20 21 | 7 11 15 | 3 12 17 | 1 6 | 10 11 12 13 14 21 | 2 | 2 | |
| Name | | | | | | | | | | | | | | | | | | | | | | | | | | |
| | | | | | | | | | | | | | | | | | | | | | | | | | | |
| | | | | | | | | | | | | | | | | | | | | | | | | | | |
| | | | | | | | | | | | | | | | | | | | | | | | | | | |
| | | | | | | | | | | | | | | | | | | | | | | | | | | |
| | | | | | | | | | | | | | | | | | | | | | | | | | | |
| | | | | | | | | | | | | | | | | | | | | | | | | | | |
| | | | | | | | | | | | | | | | | | | | | | | | | | | |
| | | | | | | | | | | | | | | | | | | | | | | | | | | |
| | | | | | | | | | | | | | | | | | | | | | | | | | | |
| | | | | | | | | | | | | | | | | | | | | | | | | | | |
| | | | | | | | | | | | | | | | | | | | | | | | | | | |
| | | | | | | | | | | | | | | | | | | | | | | | | | | |
| | | | | | | | | | | | | | | | | | | | | | | | | | | |
| | | | | | | | | | | | | | | | | | | | | | | | | | | |
| | | | | | | | | | | | | | | | | | | | | | | | | | | |
| | | | | | | | | | | | | | | | | | | | | | | | | | | |
| | | | | | | | | | | | | | | | | | | | | | | | | | | |
| | | | | | | | | | | | | | | | | | | | | | | | | | | |
| | | | | | | | | | | | | | | | | | | | | | | | | | | |
| | | | | | | | | | | | | | | | | | | | | | | | | | | |

Statements of Attainment at Level 4 (and some Level 5) not addressed in this book are covered in *Looking at our Environment*. Other levels are covered more fully in other books in the series.

# Record Keeping Chart

| Statement of Attainment | AT4 | | | | | | | | | | | | | | AT5 | | | | | | |
|---|---|---|---|---|---|---|---|---|---|---|---|---|---|---|---|---|---|---|---|---|---|
| | 3a | 3b | 3c | 3d | 4a | 4b | 4c | 4d | 4e | 5a | 5b | 5c | 5d | 5e | 3a | 3b | 4a | 4b | 4c | 5a | 5b |
| Sections in which it can be assessed<br><br>Name | | | 9 12 | 11 15 16 | | | | 9 10 | 11 14 15 16 17 | | | 12 14 | 10 | | 17 18 | 17 | 19 20 | 18 | | | 17 18 |
| | | | | | | | | | | | | | | | | | | | | | |
| | | | | | | | | | | | | | | | | | | | | | |
| | | | | | | | | | | | | | | | | | | | | | |
| | | | | | | | | | | | | | | | | | | | | | |
| | | | | | | | | | | | | | | | | | | | | | |
| | | | | | | | | | | | | | | | | | | | | | |
| | | | | | | | | | | | | | | | | | | | | | |
| | | | | | | | | | | | | | | | | | | | | | |
| | | | | | | | | | | | | | | | | | | | | | |
| | | | | | | | | | | | | | | | | | | | | | |
| | | | | | | | | | | | | | | | | | | | | | |
| | | | | | | | | | | | | | | | | | | | | | |
| | | | | | | | | | | | | | | | | | | | | | |
| | | | | | | | | | | | | | | | | | | | | | |
| | | | | | | | | | | | | | | | | | | | | | |
| | | | | | | | | | | | | | | | | | | | | | |
| | | | | | | | | | | | | | | | | | | | | | |
| | | | | | | | | | | | | | | | | | | | | | |
| | | | | | | | | | | | | | | | | | | | | | |
| | | | | | | | | | | | | | | | | | | | | | |
| | | | | | | | | | | | | | | | | | | | | | |
| | | | | | | | | | | | | | | | | | | | | | |
| | | | | | | | | | | | | | | | | | | | | | |
| | | | | | | | | | | | | | | | | | | | | | |
| | | | | | | | | | | | | | | | | | | | | | |
| | | | | | | | | | | | | | | | | | | | | | |
| | | | | | | | | | | | | | | | | | | | | | |
| | | | | | | | | | | | | | | | | | | | | | |
| | | | | | | | | | | | | | | | | | | | | | |

Statements of Attainment at Level 4 (and some Level 5) not addressed in this book are covered in *Looking at our Environment*. Other levels are covered more fully in other books in the series.

## Books and other resources

*Brazil,* Moyra Ashford (Heinemann, World in View Series) is a reference book for children aged 9–14.

*Brazil,* Marion Morrison (Macmillan, People and Places Series) reference for 9–11 year olds.

*Tomorrow's Earth,* David Bellamy (Mitchell-Beazley) – useful when studying rainforests.

*Bristol City Docks Information Pack* is available from the Bristol City Council Planning and Development Services, Brunel House, St George's Road, Bristol BS1 5UY.

Among the various guide books consulted, we have found the *Rough Guide to Brazil* (Harrap Columbus; Penguin) particularly helpful.

### Useful Addresses

*The Brazilian Embassy,* 32 Green Street, London W1A 4AT (phone 071 499 0877) can supply information, as can the larger travel agents.

*Oxfam,* 274 Banbury Road, Oxford OX2 7DZ have considerable involvement in Brazil and produce a booklet, a teaching pack (for 6th formers) and a leaflet called 'Oxfam and Brazil'.

*WaterAid's* Education Section, 1 Queen Anne's Gate, London SW1H 9BT (phone 071 233 4800) is a useful source of posters and information about water requirements world wide. They do a free fundraising pack for primary schools.

# HEINEMANN OUR WORLD GEOGRAPHY TOPICS

## KEY STAGE 1 (Levels 1–3)
Out and About
Homes and Settlements
Just Outside

## LOWER KEY STAGE 2 (Level 2, with some 3)
Our Local Community
People Live Here
Looking Around

## MIDDLE KEY STAGE 2 (Level 3, with some 4)
Here and There
Where You Live

## UPPER KEY STAGE 2 (Level 4, with some 5)
Comparing Places
Looking At Our Environment